CULTIVATING PEARLS

A CREATIVE JOURNEY OF TRANSFORMATION

CULTIVATING PEARLS

CHRISTINA DiMARI

The nonfiction imprint of
Tyndale House Publishers, Inc.

Visit Tyndale online at www.tyndale.com.

Visit Tyndale Momentum online at www.tyndalemomentum.com.

Visit the author's website at riverandpearls.org.

TYNDALE, Tyndale Momentum, and Tyndale's quill logo are registered trademarks of Tyndale House Publishers, Inc. The Tyndale Momentum logo is a trademark of Tyndale House Publishers, Inc. Tyndale Momentum is the nonfiction imprint of Tyndale House Publishers, Inc., Carol Stream, Illinois.

Cultivating Pearls

Designed by Libby Dykstra

For information about special discounts for bulk purchases, please contact Tyndale House Publishers at csresponse@tyndale.com, or call 1-800-323-9400.

ISBN 978-1-4964-4149-2

Printed in the United States of America

25 24 23 22 21 20 19
7   6   5   4   3   2   1

To

DR. LEONARD WALLMARK

12/21/31—5/15/17

For teaching me how to be like a tree with roots going down
deep into God's truth and love. Your teaching during my
college-age years changed my life. I will forever be grateful.

To

ALL THE GIRLS

who have listened and responded to the call of Jesus,
inviting you to come to the river to begin your journey of being
cultivated into a beautiful pearl. To the girls whom I have taught
these lessons to, either in class, at a retreat, or in my home, you
have inspired me and taught me as well. My heart is filled to
overflowing as I watch you listen, explore, process, and create.
The format of this book has taken shape because of my time
with you, discovering what has helped you the most. Many
of you are now reaching out to other girls either in children's
hospitals, on campus, or in your community. I believe a wave of
revival is coming over the youth and young adults in this world
who are craving an authentic walk with God. You are already
part of leading the way. I am so proud of you for reflecting the
love of God beautifully and uniquely to the world around you!

THE MEANING OF A PEARL

WHEN A SINGLE GRAIN OF SAND enters the living membrane of an oyster, the oyster becomes irritated by the foreign object. The oyster's reaction is to continually coat it with a substance called *nacre*, eventually transforming the grain of sand into a beautiful pearl.

The Latin word for pearl literally means "unique," attesting to the fact that no two pearls are identical.

You and I are like that grain of sand when we come to God. He receives us as we are, then covers us with his grace and refines us by the truth of his Word.

Through that process, he creates something beautiful in us that, each in our own unique and creative way, reflects who he is to the world around us.

CONTENTS

CONTENTS SUMMARY

A NOTE FROM CHRISTINA

THE VISION FOR THIS BOOK started after I was invited to speak at a chapel service at my alma mater, Simpson University in Northern California, during its homecoming celebration. I spent some time with Dr. Wallmark, my theology and Bible professor. During my college years, his style of teaching had greatly impacted my life and taught me not only how to know about God, but how to walk in a personal relationship with him.

Dr. Wallmark knew I had been speaking at youth and college events for several years, and that I had written books to help girls on their journeys with God. Dr. Wallmark wanted to know how this next generation of girls was doing. I shared how in my work with high school and college-age girls I could see a desire to want to know God. To grow. To learn. To love. But I could also see a disconnection between knowing the truth of God's Word and knowing how it flowed into all the parts of their lives. Even though many of them believed in God, they still felt he was very far away. I explained to my former professor that I wanted to help girls discover how to walk with God in a way that felt personal and part of their everyday lives.

Dr. Wallmark sat back in his chair and said, "I see another book coming! There is a prayer chapel down the road; it may be a good time to have a talk with God about it."

I left our time together feeling stirred inside my spirit that something was about to happen.

I entered the prayer chapel and started reading Revelation 21 and 22, which had been part of my Bible reading that month.

I would read a few verses, and then I would stop and close my eyes, imagining what the words looked like and what they were communicating to me.

The Scripture paints a picture of this beautiful river that flows from the throne of God, and I imagined Jesus in this river calling us to come to him.

As I stayed with this picture in my mind, I found myself imagining Jesus reaching for something deep down in the water. I could see golden light and beautiful blue water slightly moving as he brought his hand up to the surface.

I was curious and found myself asking him in prayer, "Jesus, what are you doing?"

His eyes were fixed on me and his light and glory flowed all over me as his simple answer found its way deep into my spirit.

"I'm cultivating pearls," he said, as his hand broke the surface of the water, revealing one of his treasures.

He held a solitary pearl before me and said, "This is Saylor. This is her story and how she is letting me transform her life, just like you did." He reached for another pearl. "This is Courtney." And another one. "This is Morgan."

Over and over, he showed me girls from all over the world. Each one trusted Jesus with her life and placed herself in his Living Water.

It was the most beautiful scene. Jesus told me each girl's name, her story, and what she had been through. He showed me how he was covering her with his grace and shaping her by the truth of his Word. The girls were like trees—firmly rooted and growing in faith and love. As each one flourished, I saw her leaves blowing off her tree and bringing hope and healing to others.

Then the picture in my mind shifted. It was as if I was looking at the whole world from a distance. I could see Jesus in the river calling the girls to come to him.

Some of the girls were close so they could hear his voice, and they were making their way to the river.

Other girls were farther away. It was as if they could hear this faint voice and were looking up, wondering where it came from, but they didn't know what to do or where to go.

Other girls were so far away that as the call went out, they could barely even hear it.

Then I imagined girls who had heard the call and come to the river going back out to help those who didn't know how to get there. Girls all over the world going out and taking other girls by the hand, until thousands upon thousands of girls are at the river and learning to experience God's love and understand his purpose for their lives.

The picture in my mind shifted again, and I felt like it was back to just me and Jesus. I asked him why he was showing me this beautiful picture and what he wanted me to do.

That's when I felt him speak to my heart about writing this book, *Cultivating Pearls*, and guiding you on this beautiful creative journey of transformation that is filled with many lessons that have shaped my own life over the years.

I humbly knelt before the River of the Water of Life and slipped my hands into the water as a symbol of my dedication to fulfill the assignment Jesus was asking me to do.

"What is the most important thing?" I asked him.

"Make It Beautiful!" he said.

I felt as if everything I was reading in Revelation 21 and 22 was painting a picture of how beautiful the Kingdom of God is, and that Jesus wanted girls to know that although the process of transformation is not always easy, it will be the most beautiful journey they can ever embark upon.

Wherever you are, I invite you now to take my hand and let me lead you to the river where your beautiful journey of transformation will begin!

A NOTE FROM MADISON

FIVE YEARS AGO, when I was a junior in high school, I was taken on a journey through the lessons in *Cultivating Pearls* where I discovered what it meant to accept Christ's invitation to come. To come to the River of the Water of Life that flows from the throne of God to be purified, empowered in the light of Christ, anointed by God as his daughter, rooted in his perfect love, and given life to shine for others.

Through this process I learned how to not only believe in God, but to make a personal connection with him. I discovered that God asks us to join him, and he gives us a purpose to be part of his Kingdom work on earth. I ended my yearlong journey by making a sacred covenant with God and dedicated my life to live within the beautiful boundaries of his Kingdom and continue to allow the truth of his Word to shape and guide my life. I dedicated my life to sharing his love with other girls so they, too, can discover how to respond to his call and come.

As I entered college, I realized so many girls were searching. They were searching for something that would fill a hole in their hearts, mend broken relationships, or bring light into something difficult they were experiencing. They were searching for meaningful friendships—who they were and who they could become. They wanted something real. Something authentic. Something lasting. Sadly, I mostly saw girls looking for what their souls longed for in places and people who left them disappointed and unfulfilled.

I knew someone who can totally and completely satisfy what their souls longed for. He did it for me. His name is Jesus. I wanted to help the girls get to know him and understand how to have a personal relationship with him.

Even though I was only a freshman in college, I asked some of the girls I met if they wanted to grow spiritually. Before I knew it, I was guiding a group of girls through the same lessons in *Cultivating Pearls* that had shaped my own life.

They listened to the call of Jesus inviting them to come. Each girl, with her own unique story, came week after week to learn and grow. Some of the girls had never read a Bible or the teachings of Jesus, while others grew up going to church but didn't know how to make their faith personal. It was the most rewarding experience to come alongside the girls and share these lessons and watch Jesus bring hope to their lives.

They learned how to walk with God in an intimate way. To take time to evaluate where they are, open their hearts and allow the truth of God's words to bring light and guidance. The creative and journaling elements of the lessons create a safe way for the girls to explore and express what they are feeling in a way that brings clarity. They love how it is a journey with God, not a program. It's not something they do and—*ta-da!*—they are done and know it all and have it all figured out. They are learning how to process, how to communicate, how to connect. They are learning how the Kingdom of God is not far away, but through their faith in Jesus, it is in their hearts.

As the girls came together each week, they were vulnerable with each other, sharing their stories and struggles, being real. They allowed each lesson to bring guidance into their lives, and I watched the beauty of God's Word bring about transformation in each of the girls over the year we met together.

I am now a senior in college, and each year I have continued to lead a group of girls through the life-changing lessons in *Cultivating Pearls*.

I receive deep satisfaction and joy by helping the girls connect with God in a personal way, break down walls they've built up, and discover truth in the midst of so many lies our society tells them. I love watching the girls experience the presence of God in the middle of chaos, discover their identity in a lost generation, and allow the love and power of Christ to transform their lives.

As I am getting ready to graduate from college, I have been praying about how I can continue to be a light for more girls.

Christina reached out to me and asked if I would come alongside her as she created this newly revised version of *Cultivating Pearls* you now hold in your hands. She asked if I would create the illustrations for each lesson that will help you process and explore. I immediately said YES, knowing it would be an opportunity to come alongside more girls as this book finds its way into your hands.

As you begin your own creative journey of transformation, I pray that the words on each page would not only speak truth to your mind, but they would soak into your heart. I pray that the Word of God would become like precious jewels that continually show you new things about the Kingdom of God. I pray that the drawings and word pictures in this book would be seen as something beautiful and will inspire you with fresh ideas to create a beautiful reflection of what is happening in your heart. I pray that your relationship with Jesus grows deep and wide, and that you will experience his love in a radical way and desire to make him the center of your life. I pray your spirit will hear Jesus calling you to come to him, and you will respond and make your way to the River of the Water of Life where you will be Purifed, Empowered, Anointed, Rooted, and filled with Life to shine for others.

You are seen. You are known. You are worth it. You are loved.

Open up your heart as you begin your own creative journey of transformation, because it is going to be a beautiful one!

TOOLS FOR YOUR JOURNEY

1. Come as You Are

Wherever you find yourself in your mind or heart or life as you hold this book in your hands, the best place to begin your journey is right where you are. The pages of this book are filled with lessons that will become tools to encourage, empower, and equip you on your journey of learning how to connect with God, grow in your faith, and discover your unique purpose in this world.

2. What You Need

Your Bible, a *Cultivating Pearls* book, a bunch of colored pencils, and a writing pen. In addition to practical items, you will need consistency, an open heart, and a desire to grow.

3. Do I Need to Be Creative?

When I use the word *creative,* I am not referring to being an artist. I use the word *creative* to define a unique way of processing your thoughts, ideas, and feelings through words, drawings, and color. I believe we all have a creative outlet, but how that flows out of each of us is in a very unique way. So the answer is, you already are creative. This book will inspire you to discover how.

4. Discover

Every lesson is created to flow into the next, bringing the whole journey together in a beautiful way at the end. Everything you do on the way will become your own reflection of discovering how to listen and respond to the truth of God's Word as it transforms your life.

5. Express Yourself

After I share a lesson I will ask a variety of questions. This is not the kind of book where you just read something and fill in the blank. This is a book of lessons shared and questions asked, and you go on your own personal creative journey to answer them. Some of you may be more inclined to write or journal. I encourage you to also try to sketch something to get a visual to go with your words. Some of you may be more inclined to draw. I encourage you to also add words that describe what you are drawing.

6. Thoughts and Emotions

When we write, we are primarily using our minds to express our thoughts. When we take time to consider what drawing or visual may represent what we are thinking, we tap into our hearts.

7. Transformation in Mind and Heart

When we read a verse of Scripture, it is important to understand what we are reading so it has the power to transform our minds. When we think about a verse of Scripture and try to come up with a visual way to illustrate this verse and then find ourselves in that picture, it helps the transformation flow into the depths of our hearts as well. My hope for you is that you will not only know about the Kingdom of God, but that the beauty of the Kingdom of God will become the very center of your heart and flow into all the pieces of your life.

8. Revelation 21 and 22

Throughout your journey there will be several times I ask you to reflect on a passage in Revelation 21 and 22. These chapters are included on the following pages in case you don't happen to have your Bible with you.

REVELATION 21

Then I saw a new heaven and a new earth, for the old heaven and the old earth had disappeared. And the sea was also gone. And I saw the holy city, the new Jerusalem, coming down from God out of heaven like a bride beautifully dressed for her husband.

I heard a loud shout from the throne, saying, "Look, God's home is now among his people! He will live with them, and they will be his people. God himself will be with them. He will wipe every tear from their eyes, and there will be no more death or sorrow or crying or pain. All these things are gone forever."

And the one sitting on the throne said, "Look, I am making everything new!" And then he said to me, "Write this down, for what I tell you is trustworthy and true." And he also said, "It is finished! I am the Alpha and the Omega—the Beginning and the End. To all who are thirsty I will give freely from the springs of the water of life. All who are victorious will inherit all these blessings, and I will be their God, and they will be my children.

"But cowards, unbelievers, the corrupt, murderers, the immoral, those who practice witchcraft, idol worshipers, and all liars—their fate is in the fiery lake of burning sulfur. This is the second death."

Then one of the seven angels who held the seven bowls containing the seven last plagues came and said to me, "Come with me! I will show you the bride, the wife of the Lamb."

So he took me in the Spirit to a great, high mountain, and he showed me the holy city, Jerusalem, descending out of heaven from God. It shone with the glory of God and sparkled like a precious stone—like jasper as clear as crystal. The city wall was broad and high, with twelve gates guarded by twelve angels. And the names of the twelve tribes of Israel were written on the gates. There were three gates on each side—east, north, south, and west. The wall of the city had twelve foundation stones, and on them were written the names of the twelve apostles of the Lamb.

The angel who talked to me held in his hand a gold measuring stick to measure the city, its gates, and its wall. When he measured it, he found it was a square, as wide as it was long. In fact, its length and width and height were each 1,400 miles. Then he measured the walls and found them to be 216 feet thick (according to the human standard used by the angel).

The wall was made of jasper, and the city was pure gold, as clear as glass. The wall of the city was built on foundation stones inlaid with twelve precious stones: the first was jasper, the second sapphire, the third agate, the fourth emerald, the fifth onyx, the sixth carnelian, the seventh chrysolite, the eighth beryl, the ninth topaz, the tenth chrysoprase, the eleventh jacinth, the twelfth amethyst.

The twelve gates were made of pearls—each gate from a single pearl! And the main street was pure gold, as clear as glass.

I saw no temple in the city, for the Lord God Almighty and the Lamb are its temple. And the city has no need of sun or moon, for the glory of God illuminates the city, and the Lamb is its light. The nations will walk in its light, and the kings of the world will enter the city in all their glory. Its gates will never be closed at the end of day because there is no night there. And all the nations will bring their glory and honor into the city. Nothing evil will be allowed to enter, nor anyone who practices shameful idolatry and dishonesty—but only those whose names are written in the Lamb's Book of Life.

REVELATION 22

Then the angel showed me a river with the water of life, clear as crystal, flowing from the throne of God and of the Lamb. It flowed down the center of the main street. On each side of the river grew a tree of life, bearing twelve crops of fruit, with a fresh crop each month. The leaves were used for medicine to heal the nations.

No longer will there be a curse upon anything. For the throne of God and of the Lamb will be there, and his servants will worship him. And they will see his face, and his name will be written on their foreheads. And there will be no night there—no need for lamps or sun—for the Lord God will shine on them. And they will reign forever and ever.

Then the angel said to me, "Everything you have heard and seen is trustworthy and true. The Lord God, who inspires his prophets, has sent his angel to tell his servants what will happen soon."

"Look, I am coming soon! Blessed are those who obey the words of prophecy written in this book."

I, John, am the one who heard and saw all these things. And when I heard and saw them, I fell down to worship at the feet of the angel who showed them to me. But he said, "No, don't worship me. I am a servant of God, just like you and your brothers the prophets, as well as all who obey what is written in this book. Worship only God!"

Then he instructed me, "Do not seal up the prophetic words in this book, for the time is near. Let the one who is doing harm continue to do harm; let the one who is vile continue to be vile; let the one who is righteous continue to live righteously; let the one who is holy continue to be holy."

"Look, I am coming soon, bringing my reward with me to repay all people according to their deeds. I am the Alpha and the Omega, the First and the Last, the Beginning and the End."

Blessed are those who wash their robes. They will be permitted to enter through the gates of the city and eat the fruit from the tree of life. Outside the city are the dogs—the sorcerers, the sexually immoral, the murderers, the idol worshipers, and all who love to live a lie.

"I, Jesus, have sent my angel to give you this message for the churches. I am both the source of David and the heir to his throne. I am the bright morning star."

The Spirit and the bride say, "Come." Let anyone who hears this say, "Come." Let anyone who is thirsty come. Let anyone who desires drink freely from the water of life. And I solemnly declare to everyone who hears the words of prophecy written in this book: If anyone adds anything to what is written here, God will add to that person the plagues described in this book. And if anyone removes any of the words from this book of prophecy, God will remove that person's share in the tree of life and in the holy city that are described in this book.

He who is the faithful witness to all these things says, "Yes, I am coming soon!"

Amen! Come, Lord Jesus!

May the grace of the Lord Jesus be with God's holy people.

LET'S BEGIN

YOUR

Journey

Purified

PURIFIED IN THE RIVER OF THE WATER OF LIFE
Called, Loved, Accepted, Forgiven, Whole

THE RIVER OF LIFE

Then the angel showed me THE RIVER of the water of life, bright as crystal, flowing from the throne of God and of the Lamb through the middle of the street of the city; also, on either side of the river, THE TREE OF LIFE with its twelve kinds of fruit, yielding its fruit each month. The LEAVES of the tree were for the HEALING of the nations.

REVELATION 22:1-2, ESV (EMPHASIS ADDED)

AN INVITATION TO COME

The Spirit and the Bride say, "Come." And let the one who hears say, "Come." And let the one who is thirsty come; let the one who desires take the water of life without price.

REVELATION 22:17, ESV

The beginning to your beautiful creative journey of transformation starts with an invitation from Jesus!

PREPARING YOUR HEART

Worship

To worship God is to celebrate God's perfection. Much of the time we spend our time in prayer and gratitude for things pertaining to ourselves. Worship helps us shift our focus upward, to God alone. Focus your attention upon God your Father and celebrate the wonder of who he is.

> Worship is to feel in your heart and express in some appropriate manner a humbling but delightful sense of admiring awe and astonished wonder and overpowering love in the presence of the most ancient Mystery, that majesty which philosophers call the First Cause but which we call Our Father Which Art in Heaven.
>
> A.W. TOZER

> Worship prepares my heart to listen and learn from the truth of God's Word and feel his presence by my side. Worship is declaring the goodness and glory of God. Sometimes it helps me to put on worship music[1] and I speak the truth of the words, and other times I worship God with words that flow from my heart. This establishes an environment where I am in a quiet place with Jesus and he does the inner work of transforming my life like a pearl.
>
> HANNAH HART, A COLLEGE STUDENT LEADER

---

[1] You can find a list of recommended worship songs on our website, River + Pearls | RiverandPearls.org

Prayer

The process of creating your pearl starts with a single grain of sand entering the living membrane of an oyster. In spiritual terms, this is an invitation for you to come to God in prayer. Prayer is communication between you and God. This will become the foundation from which new growth in your life will be cultivated. Prayer forms a partnership between you and God where you can be honest about all that is in your heart and mind. This opens up an invitation for the Spirit of God to flow into the deeper places of who you are. Through prayer you get to know each other. You talk. He listens. He talks. You listen. You ask him questions. He asks you questions. You surrender. He shapes. You reevaluate. He molds.

Jesus is inviting you to come to this beautiful River of Life that flows from God's throne to receive what you need for your journey. Whether you feel close or far away, the lessons in this Purified section will help you hear the Spirit of God calling you to come to him and be touched by his love. No matter what your background or your past or current situation is like, I encourage you to stop and listen.

Read and meditate on Revelation 21 and 22 on pages xxiii–xxvi.

When I think of where God is, based on Revelation 22:1, I think of the mountains, where pure, clean water flows from the purest source.

THE RIVER OF LIFE

Reflect on these verses again:

THE RIVER OF LIFE

> Then the angel showed me THE RIVER of the water of life, bright as crystal, flowing from the throne of God and of the Lamb through the middle of the street of the city; also, on either side of the river, THE TREE OF LIFE with its twelve kinds of fruit, yielding its fruit each month. The LEAVES of the tree were for the HEALING of the nations.
>
> REVELATION 22:1-2, ESV (EMPHASIS ADDED)

AN INVITATION TO COME

> The Spirit and the Bride say, "Come." And let the one who hears say, "Come." And let the one who is thirsty come; let the one who desires take the water of life without price.
>
> REVELATION 22:17, ESV

Look at the picture to your right. Imagine Jesus is at the river calling you to come to him. Where do you imagine you are?

Place yourself in the picture either with a drawing or with a symbol of a pearl representing your life. Add anything else that comes to mind.

Color in the drawing, choosing colors that reflect how you feel.

Write the five key words for this lesson somewhere in the picture: *Called, Loved, Accepted, Forgiven, Whole.*

Create

Express yourself in your own unique way on this spread.

When you close your eyes and imagine hearing Jesus calling you to come to the river, what comes to your mind or how do you feel in your heart?

Draw something that reflects what you imagine and feel. Place yourself somewhere in the picture.

Write five words that represent your picture.

Write a prayer to God asking for what you desire as you begin your journey.

_____

_____

_____

_____

_____

_____

_____

_____

_____

_____

_____

_____

_____

_____

_____

_____

MAKING A PERSONAL CONNECTION

The previous lesson was focused on introducing you to the beauty of the Kingdom of God. As you meditated on the verses in Revelation 21 and 22, it was my hope that you could imagine the beautiful river that flows from the throne of God. That you would stop and listen and hear Jesus calling you in your heart to come to him.

Over the years, I have noticed many girls feeling far from God. It was not always because they were choosing to live apart from God's ways but somewhere, deep in their spirit, they felt as if he was so far away and it was up to them to somehow reach him. It seemed impossible. They wanted to know him. They just didn't know how.

The good news of the gospel is that we do not need to be the ones to reach out to God and try to find a way to get to him. He has come to us through his Son, Jesus Christ.

FOR *God loved the world* SO MUCH

THAT HE GAVE HIS ONE AND ONLY SON,

SO THAT EVERYONE WHO

BELIEVES IN HIM WILL NOT PERISH

but have eternal life.

John 3:16

It is through your faith and belief in Jesus that the beauty of the Kingdom of God begins to transform your life.

Wherever you are in your life right now, take a moment to close your eyes and imagine what you learned about the Kingdom of God in this session. When you believe in Jesus, he brings the beauty of his Kingdom into your heart.

On the following spread, use the left side to write a prayer and/or journal your thoughts.

Color the picture on the right side, thinking about the words in this lesson.

The beautiful blue river is like a symbol of the Holy Spirit flowing like water into the cracks and crevices of your heart to bring comfort, healing, and peace.

The mountains represent God our Father. There is a mystery to God and still many things to search for and discover about him. God is always calling out to us, inviting us to explore more about him and give us new perspectives.

The sunrise casting light over the mountain peaks represents Jesus, the Light of the World. He asks us to follow him, and he provides a path for us to know where to go and how to live according to his Kingdom.

Create

> He has planted eternity in the human heart.
>
> ECCLESIASTES 3:11

Reflect on everything you have read about the Kingdom of God, your belief in Christ, and where you feel you are when thinking about your heart.

On this page, write a prayer or journal your thoughts.

Color the picture to your right and feel free to add to the picture.

_____

_____

_____

_____

_____

_____

_____

_____

_____

_____

_____

_____

_____

_____

_____

_____

_____

_____

_____

FOR THE LORD GOD IS A

sun and shield:

THE LORD WILL GIVE

grace and glory:

NO GOOD THING WILL HE

WITHHOLD FROM THOSE THAT

walk uprightly.

Psalm 84:11, KJV

EXCHANGING GIFTS WITH GOD

The first time I ever did a gift exchange with God, I happened to be having my quiet time with him one morning during the Christmas holidays. As I sat in my favorite blue chair by the Christmas tree, I began talking to God about some things I had on my heart.

I felt like I heard this whisper in my heart, "Give it to me." I knew what he meant. He wanted me to give him everything I was worried about or felt I needed.

I looked at all the presents under the tree and realized he was asking me to give him something tangible, too. I went downstairs and found a gold box, filled it with something that represented what I was giving him, and wrote a long letter explaining what I was giving and why. I tied a long ribbon around the box, finishing it with a bow, and put it under the tree.

Part of me felt good that I did it. I gave it to him. But then I realized I gave him something that I was worried about. What kind of gift was that? Certainly not a good one.

I asked him again, "What can I give you that is beautiful?" The answer that came to my heart was, "You gave me what I asked for. I will make something beautiful out of what you gave me. You will see over time."

After I was at peace with the gift I had given, I felt like he was asking me what I wanted, as if he was going to give me a gift as well. I wanted to make sure whatever I asked for was coming from a truth in his Word, so I opened my Bible and searched for a Scripture that represented what I felt I needed for my journey at that time.

As I continued to explore God's Word, I came to realize that there were deep wells of water I could drink from when I was thirsty. In time, I also saw how he took everything I gave him and made something beautiful from my offering.

He will do the same for you!

EXCHANGING GIFTS WITH GOD

Ask Jesus, "What would you like that I can give you?"

Jesus answers, "I would like for you to give me . . ."

_____

_____

_____

_____

_____

_____

When I present a gift, I usually imagine laying it beside the river or in the river; the river is a symbolic image for me of where Jesus is.

Do whatever seems to flow naturally for you as you pray. It may take some time to listen. After you know what you are going to give, draw your picture.

On the page to your right is an example for you to color to get your creative juices flowing.

On the following spread, you will have an entire space to express with words and a drawing what you are giving.

Take some time to be still in prayer and worship. Before you start creating, I encourage you to put on some worship music and take some time to pray and listen to what comes to your heart and mind.

GIVING YOUR GIFT

Write a prayer or share your thoughts on what you are giving to Jesus.

_____

_____

_____

_____

_____

_____

_____

_____

_____

_____

_____

_____

_____

_____

_____

_____

_____

_____

_____

_____

_____

_____

Draw or sketch
a picture, using
one or more colors
to reflect what you
are feeling.

EXCHANGING GIFTS WITH GOD

Jesus is asking you, "What do you need from me?"
You answer, "I need . . ."

Keep this request connected to the gift you offered Jesus on the previous page. Example: I gave God my pearls. Then he asked me, "Now that you have given me your gift, what do you need from me so that I can fill you up with what you need from my Word?"

When I was younger, I said I needed wisdom from other women. At times. he will use people to touch us and come alongside us, but first, he wants to pour the water of his Word into us. This is not asking Jesus for a wish list or a dream list. It is a deep-in-your-soul-what-you-need request that his Word can touch.

On the page to your right is an example for you to color to get your creative juices flowing.

Take some time to be still in prayer and worship before you start creating. Reflect on the Scripture and lesson. Listen in prayer. Imagine where you are. What are you thinking and feeling? How is this lesson meeting you where you are and encouraging you on your journey? Color the page on the right and add anything to make it personal.

Then on the next two pages, you will have an entire spread to express with words and a drawing what you are receiving.

RECEIVING YOUR GIFT

Write a prayer or share your thoughts on what you are receiving from Jesus.

_____

_____

_____

_____

_____

_____

_____

_____

_____

_____

_____

_____

_____

_____

_____

_____

_____

_____

_____

_____

_____

_____

Draw or sketch a picture, using one or more colors to reflect what you are feeling.

LESSONS FROM A STAR

Creation is part of God's general revelation, and it testifies to God's existence. Through creation, he often reveals himself to us.

> They know the truth about God because he has made it obvious to them. For ever since the world was created, people have seen the earth and sky. Through everything God made, they can clearly see his invisible qualities— his eternal power and divine nature. So they have no excuse for not knowing God.
>
> ROMANS 1:19-20

God often reveals himself through the physical world to communicate things about himself that we may not already know. He does this often on a very personal level with each one of us, sometimes teaching us important spiritual lessons through the work of his hands. The lessons we learn from nature often become our symbols, reminding us of what God is like, what he has done for us, and what he is teaching us.

When Israel crossed the Jordan River into the Promised Land, God gave Joshua the following instructions:

> Now choose twelve men, one from each tribe. Tell them, "Take twelve stones from the very place where the priests are standing in the middle of the Jordan. Carry them out and pile them up at the place where you will camp tonight."
>
> JOSHUA 4:2-3

The stones were to serve as a reminder to the Israelites.

> We will use these stones to build a memorial. In the future your children
> will ask you, "What do these stones mean?" Then you can tell them, "They
> remind us that the Jordan River stopped flowing when the Ark of the
> LORD's Covenant went across." These stones will stand as a memorial among
> the people of Israel forever.
>
> JOSHUA 4:6-7

When God uses things in his creation to mold us and teach us lessons, these often become symbols for us to remember what we have learned. They become our own stones of remembrance of how God worked in our life.

The image of a starfish will always remind me to stay connected to my life source so that all the pieces of my life are restored, healthy, whole, and able to shine light for others.

There are many lessons I have learned from God's creation over the years that I will share with you throughout this journey. We will also explore the ways God has already revealed himself to you, define the lessons you are learning, and what you want to remember as you go on from here. Because this session is about being purified in the Water of Life, the symbol from nature I think of is a starfish.

It all began when I was a young child, often gazing at the nighttime sky and wondering if God lived there. I guess I thought he should live there because it all seemed so beautiful and full of light. But at that time of my life all that light felt so very far away. This story I wrote reflects my thoughts and opens up the pathway through which God began to reveal himself to me.

A long time ago, the nighttime sky was filled with bright shining stars. All we had to do was look up to their light to help us find our way. There were so many stars to look up to that no one ever got lost. Then one day some of the stars forgot how to shine for each other.

One by one, many of them broke and fell from the sky. They landed in the sea. Some people call them starfish, but they're really ocean stars. They're on a journey to learn how to get put back together again. All of the struggles they endure and the lessons they have learned help them form a pearl of light, deep in the center of their star. Once they find their light, they turn back into a star, shining for others the way they were meant to.

So if you ever find an ocean star, be sure to be kind and gentle.

It is trying to find its way home.

It wasn't until my freshman year in college that someone first shared with me that there is a connection between God, the stars, and me. A girl from school invited me to church, and the pastor read this:

> Look up into the heavens. Who created all the stars? He brings them out like an army, one after another, calling each by its name. Because of his great power and incomparable strength, not a single one is missing.
>
> ISAIAH 40:26

"Have you ever looked at the nighttime sky and wondered if God thinks about you?" the pastor asked. "He knows each of the stars in the sky and knows them each by name. He knows you. He knows your name. He wants you to know him, too. That's why he sent his Son, Jesus, the Bright Morning Star, to give his life, so that you can find your way home and become a child of God."

> I, Jesus, have sent my angel to give you this message for the churches. I am both the source of David and the heir to his throne. I am the bright morning star.
>
> REVELATION 22:16

That night I knelt down and closed my eyes to receive God's gift. All I could see before me was a cross and, in that moment, I believed Jesus was real. I asked him to help me get to know him and what to do next.

I wanted to give something back to God. In my mind's eye, I imagined giving him my star.

> God made my life complete when I placed all the pieces before him.
>
> PSALM 18:24, MSG

I had learned that when an ocean star is washed up on shore, it hardens and dies. But if it is connected to its life source, the ocean, it becomes moldable and alive. It doesn't matter if the ocean star is broken or bruised or had pieces completely cut off. As long as it gets back to the water, it will slowly regenerate and become whole. When I let the Living Water of God's words and Spirit flow through me, little by little I began to feel changed on the inside.

> He alone is my rock and my salvation, my fortress where I will never be shaken.
>
> PSALM 62:2

It didn't mean everything was going to be easy, but I wasn't out there in the middle of the ocean any longer, being tossed around by the waves. In reality, when starfish are tossed around in the waves by a violent storm, the ones that survive are the ones that attach themselves securely to a rock.

On the bottom of each starfish are tiny orange eyespots. The starfish cannot see like we do, but it is able to navigate by its keen sense of light and dark. The Kingdom of God is light. Outside of the Kingdom of God's boundaries is darkness. I wanted to be "in tune" to light and dark so I could be sure to stay "inside" the light and protection of God's rule.

I have learned how important it is for me to be my own unique self and not try to be like anyone else.

Healing is, by definition, the process of making whole. It is remembering who we truly are, remembering who we are in Christ. God does this work in us so that we can live out our lives from this place of wholeness.

On the following pages you will begin to discover meaning from some of these lessons for yourself. As you do, I pray that you will open your heart to the Lord and allow him into all the places of your heart.

May you look up at the nighttime sky and notice each star's shimmering light and be reminded that just as he calls the stars by name, he calls your name too.

When the thrashing waves of life threaten to take you down, may you find your rock and hold on tight!

May you feel the Holy Spirit come alongside you as a friend, offering you comfort and guidance. As you allow him to flow into the cracks and crevices of your life, may he heal any part of your life that needs his touch.

I pray that you will become a bright light in this world, shining for others to also find their way home to God.

Create

> Look up into the heavens. Who created all the stars? He brings them out
> . . . one after another, calling each by its name. Because of his great power
> and incomparable strength, not a single one is missing.
>
> ISAIAH 40:26

- When you look up at the stars, what do you think about?
- Do you feel close to God or far away?
- Do you wonder if he thinks about you?
- Do you feel like a broken star that fell from the sky?
- Do you feel like a starfish trying to find your way home?

God knows each of the stars in the sky and knows them each by name. He knows you. He knows your name. He wants you to know him, too. That's why he sent his Son, Jesus, the Bright Morning Star, to give his life, so that you can find your way home to become a child of God.

Whether you are just now getting to know Jesus, or you have been following him for a while, take a moment to reflect on how you would answer the questions above.

On the following page, create a drawing that represents how you would answer the questions on this page. Think about where you are and where you want to be. Write a short prayer and date the page.

Create

> God made my life complete when I placed all the pieces before him.
> PSALM 18:24, MSG

What are the "pieces" of your life?

_____

_____

_____

Do you have any pieces that feel broken, bruised, or totally cut off?

_____

_____

_____

Are you ready to place these pieces of your life in the water?

_____

_____

_____

On the page to your right . . .

Take some time to be still in prayer and worship before you start creating. Reflect on the Scripture and lesson. Listen in prayer. Imagine where you are. What are you thinking and feeling? How is this lesson meeting you where you are and encouraging you on your journey? Color the page and add anything to make it personal.

Create

> Don't be afraid, for I am with you. Don't be discouraged, for I am your
> God. I will strengthen you and help you. I will hold you up with my
> victorious right hand.
>
> ISAIAH 41:10

> Don't worry about anything; instead, pray about everything. Tell God what
> you need, and thank him for all he has done. Then you will experience
> God's peace, which exceeds anything we can understand. His peace will
> guard your hearts and minds as you live in Christ Jesus.
>
> PHILIPPIANS 4: 6-7

> When I am afraid, I will put my trust in you.
>
> PSALM 56:3

When have you ever felt tossed around by the waves, without an anchor to
hold on to?

Use the lines below to write your thoughts.

On the page to your right, color the picture and add words to illustrate
what you feel when you think about being tossed around in the waves.

_____

_____

_____

_____

_____

_____

_____

_____

Create

> He alone is my rock and my salvation, my fortress where I will never be shaken.
>
> PSALM 62:2

Write words that describe how Jesus is our Rock. Example: He is dependable; He is faithful.

When you feel overwhelmed, how can you cling to Jesus as your Rock? Use the space below to write three ways you can cling to Jesus and how that will affect how you think and feel.

On the page to your right, color the picture and add words to illustrate what you feel when thinking about holding on to Jesus.

_____

_____

_____

_____

_____

_____

_____

_____

_____

_____

_____

_____

_____

AND NOW, DEAR BROTHERS AND SISTERS,

ONE FINAL THING.

FIX YOUR THOUGHTS ON

WHAT IS TRUE,

AND HONORABLE,

AND RIGHT,

AND PURE,

AND LOVELY,

AND ADMIRABLE.

Think about things that are excellent and worthy of praise.

Philippians 4:8

One day I walked into a shop that carried starfish-shaped stars made out of glass. Each one was a different color. Some were clear and you could see right through them, while others were blue, green, even brown. I was curious about why and how each one formed a unique color. What I discovered shaped my life!

I was told that when a glass starfish shape is placed in pure water, it takes on the color of the water it is placed in. The same goes for the other colors. When one is placed in brown water, the star becomes brown.

As I was growing as a believer in Christ, I could see so many people concerned about following rules and becoming perfect on the outside, so they could somehow feel like they were good enough based on their own efforts.

This lesson taught me to focus my attention on what type of water I was placing every part of my life in. If my life was in the pure water that flows from the throne of God and of the Lamb as described in Revelation 22, then my whole life would reflect that water as it made its way from my inside to my outside.

As I put Christ at the center of my star, I discovered how to allow his authority and love to flow into all parts of my life. Spiritually. Mentally. Emotionally. Physically. Relationally. He was no longer a category of my life. I wanted him to be the center of it.

Create

Use color and words to describe below what your star would look and feel like if it was placed in water that was NOT pure.

For each part of your life, write a word that describes how you feel about each piece of your star in this water.

- Spiritually: How you connect with God.
- Mentally: How you think.
- Emotionally: How you feel.
- Relationally: How you relate to and treat others.
- Physically: How you relate to and treat your own body.

This is a good time to reflect on the holiness of God.

_____

_____

_____

_____

_____

_____

_____

_____

_____

_____

_____

_____

_____

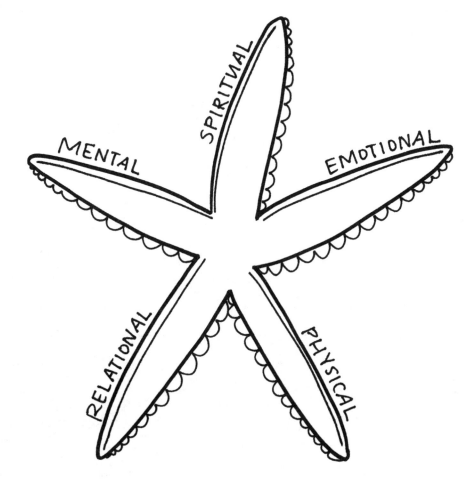

Create

Use color and words to describe below what your star would look and feel like if it was placed in water that is pure.

For each part of your life, write a word that describes how you feel about each piece of your star in this pure water.

- Spiritually: How you connect with God.
- Mentally: How you think.
- Emotionally: How you feel.
- Relationally: How you relate to and treat others.
- Physically: How you relate to and treat your own body.

This is a good time to reflect on the holiness of God.

_____

_____

_____

_____

_____

_____

_____

_____

_____

_____

_____

_____

_____

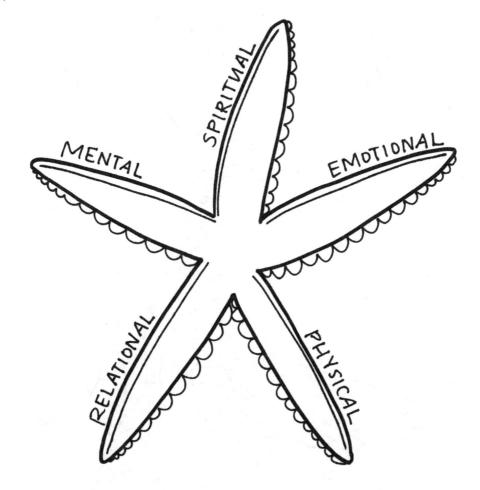

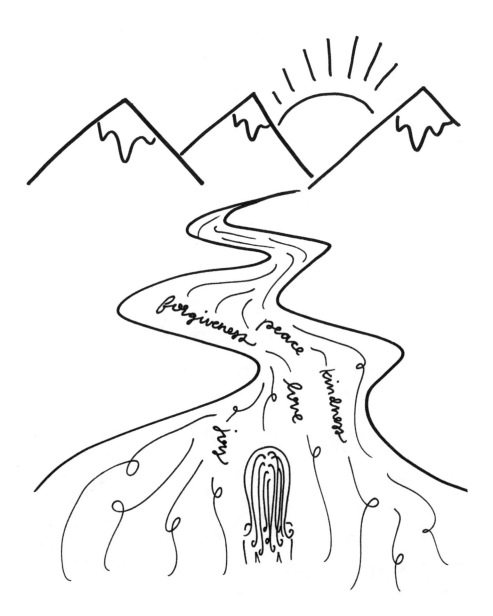

Let Go

Use the following page to draw what you want to LET GO of in your life right now. Think about everything you discovered in this Purified session. Imagine you are in the River of the Water of Life, letting go of everything you do not want to define your life going forward.

Use this page to get your thoughts out.

On the page to your right, create a visual with drawing, color, words, a prayer, and date the page.

Receive

Use the following page to draw what you want to RECEIVE in your life right now. Imagine you are in the River of the Water of Life, receiving everything you need from God your Father, through Jesus Christ, and the power of the Holy Spirit.

Use this page to get your thoughts out.

On the page to your right, create a visual with drawing, color, words, a prayer, and date the page.

Reflect on what you experienced or discovered during your Purified session as you think about each of these words.

CALLED

_____

_____

_____

LOVED

_____

_____

_____

ACCEPTED

_____

_____

_____

FORGIVEN

_____

_____

_____

WHOLE

_____

_____

_____

Empowered

E MPOWERED IN THE LIGHT OF CHRIST
Evaluate, Freedom, Forgiveness, Friendships, New

And He who sits on the throne said, "Behold, I am making all things new!"

REVELATION 21:5, NASB

Jesus spoke to the people once more and said, "I am the light of the world. If you follow me, you won't have to walk in darkness, because you will have the light that leads to life."

JOHN 8:12

As you respond to Jesus' invitation to follow him, you will be empowered to live your life released from the chains of your past and be set free to be who he created you to be.

A time to review:

PURIFIED IN THE RIVER OF THE WATER OF LIFE.
Called, Loved, Accepted, Forgiven, Whole.

The next part of your journey:

As you discover how to follow Christ and allow his light to shine into your life, you will be set free from anything that holds you back from becoming all that God designed you to be.

Sometimes things we have experienced have a way of defining how we see ourselves. When we enter into the light of Christ, we see clearly who we are based on how he sees us.

Read and meditate on Revelation 21 and 22 in your Bible or on pages xxiii–xxvi. Use an orange pencil to underline every verse that has to do with light in the Kingdom of God.

On the picture to your right, color the drawing, choosing colors that bring to life how you imagine this scene.

Add words to the picture from what you read in Revelation 21 and 22 that spoke of light.

Place yourself in the picture either with a drawing or with a symbol of a pearl representing your life.

Write the five key words for this lesson somewhere in the picture: *Evaluate, Freedom, Forgiveness, Friendships, New.*

THE TRUTH WILL SET YOU FREE

When the light of Christ is allowed to shine into our darkness, the darkness will not overcome the light. His truth tears down all the lies that have become strongholds and keep us chained to our past experiences. It's important to take some time to identify these things.

Christ wants to break every chain that holds you captive to lies and release you to live in the freedom of his truth. For the following questions, use a separate notebook if you need more room to write your answers and get your thoughts out.

What memories need healing?

_____

_____

What burdens need to be lifted?

_____

_____

Think of the parts of your life that are holding you back as a chain of links. If you were to give each link a name, what words would you use? For example: Loneliness. Anger. Bitterness. Guilt. Fear. Doubt. Jealousy. Shame. Rejection.

On the drawing to your right, use the words listed above to give each chain link a name. Use color(s) to define how you feel. Use the blank space to write a prayer asking Jesus to set you free. Date the page.

Reflect on what Jesus says:

I am the way, and the truth, and the life.

JOHN 14:6

And you will know the truth, and the truth will set you free.

JOHN 8:32

One of the heaviest chains that can hold us back is unforgiveness. Depending on the circumstances, it is not always easy to forgive. The truth of the matter is, it can be the hardest thing in the world for some people to do.

When you forgive someone, you're not telling them what they did is not bad. It may be bad. Forgiveness doesn't validate the wrong or wish for a reconciliation that cannot be had or should not be had. By forgiving someone, you're simply telling them that you are not going to hold their failures or actions against you any longer.

There was a time in my life when I struggled with forgiving someone, and I reached out in prayer to ask Jesus to help me. As I opened my eyes, I noticed a butterfly fluttering right outside my window. As I gazed at the beautiful, vibrant colors of its wings, the butterfly suddenly froze in midflight. I rushed to the window to get a closer look. Its delicate wings had become entangled in a spider web. I rushed outside, grabbed a stick, and carefully set it free.

As I watched the butterfly fly up into the sky, I felt like Jesus was asking me to do the same thing for the person I was struggling to forgive. Although it was not easy, I went back in prayer and visualized myself setting this person free. As I did, I suddenly realized . . . the butterfly wasn't the person I was forgiving. It was me.

On the page to your right, think about someone you are ready to forgive and draw a picture with words to illustrate how you feel.

LIFE-GIVING RELATIONSHIPS

As you have been spending time evaluating your life, you probably noticed that some of your good experiences were connected to healthy relationships, and some of your not-so-positive experiences were connected to unhealthy relationships. That is why we're going to spend some time looking at what healthy relationships and boundaries look like.

As you go on your journey, you get to choose whom you travel with. You don't have to stay around people who put you down or lead you down paths you don't want to go on. It is important to surround yourself with people who are life givers.

We are not meant to travel alone, but it is a sort of art to find the right kind of people who will add value to your life, as well as you adding value to theirs. Keep on the lookout. As you travel along, you never know whom you are going to meet.

Signs of life-giving people

- They respect you for who you are and don't try to change you.
- They give you space and honor you as a person.
- They encourage you.
- They want you to succeed.

Signs of life-stealing people

- They put you down.
- They are manipulative and lay guilt trips on you.
- They demand their own way.
- They want what's best for themselves.

Take a good look at the descriptions of both types of people and be honest with yourself. In your friendships and relationships, do you give life?

_____

_____

What friends give life to you?

_____

_____

How do each of your friends give life to you, and how do you give life to them?

_____

_____

Which of your family members give life to you?

_____

_____

How do each of your family members give life to you, and how do you give life to them?

_____

_____

Is there any relationship that you currently have that is not healthy for you? If so, what changes can you make?

_____

_____

MAY GOD HIMSELF, THE GOD OF PEACE,

SANCTIFY YOU THROUGH AND THROUGH.

MAY YOUR WHOLE

spirit, soul and body

BE KEPT BLAMELESS

AT THE COMING OF OUR

LORD JESUS CHRIST.

1 Thessalonians 5:23, NIV

I encourage you to put God at the very center of your life. He will bring PEACE because he *is* peace.

On the page to your right, illustrate what it would look like if God were the center of your life bringing peace.

Then add the other relationships you want to have in your life around that.

For example, you can use the image of a heart with God at the center, bringing peace. Then, list the people whom you feel safe with somewhere in the heart. Any relationships that are not life-giving to you may be put outside the heart. This is just an example to give you something to consider as you come up with your own idea.

THE LIGHT OF THE WORLD

Reflect on this verse:

> Jesus spoke to the people once more and said, "I am the light of the world.
> If you follow me, you won't have to walk in darkness, because you will have
> the light that leads to life."
>
> JOHN 8:12

Prayer and Worship

Take some time to be still before God in prayer and worship. Think about everything you have just processed.

As you close your eyes in prayer, imagine you are standing by the River of the Water of Life. All of your chains are at your feet. You have forgiven those who have hurt you. You have taken time to think about your relationships and who you want to travel with from here.

Imagine that Jesus, the Light of the World, has come to stand beside you. What do you see him doing with your chains? What do you see him doing in your heart, knowing you are forgiving those who have hurt you? What is he asking you to do in any of the relationships that you currently have?

He is asking you to take his hand, and he leads you into the water to be cleansed. Take some time to visualize what is happening there.

On the page to your right, use a drawing and words to illustrate what you felt from your experience in prayer and worship.

A LIGHT TO MY PATH

Jesus leads you by the hand back to the shore, and you are engulfed in his Light. He asks you a simple, but life-changing, question: Will you follow me?

He shows you a path that starts at the river and begins to wind its way up to the top of a beautiful mountain range. With each step you take, he will give you what you need for your journey and deep in your spirit, making all things new.

Circle the words that you want to define your life going forward.

Acceptance	Caring	Kindness	Faithfulness
Community	Creativity	Joy	Patience
Family	Forgiveness	Strength	Courage
Freedom	Gentleness	Purity	Respect
Grace	Inspired	Love	Peace

On the page to your right:

Take some time to be still in prayer and worship before you start creating. Reflect on the Scripture and lesson. Listen in prayer. Imagine where you are. What are you thinking and feeling? How is this lesson meeting you where you are and encouraging you on your journey?

Write the words you circled somewhere in the picture. Color the drawing, choosing colors that bring to life the way you imagine this scene when you are in prayer.

Create

> Your word is a lamp to guide my feet and a light for my path.
>
> PSALM 119:105

How do you know the difference between light and dark?

_____

_____

What are the characteristics of light?

_____

_____

How can God's Word be a light to your path?

_____

_____

In what areas of your life do you feel darkness that you are ready to allow the light of God to shine into?

_____

_____

On the page to your right:

Take some time to be still in prayer and worship before you start creating. Reflect on the Scripture and lesson. Listen in prayer. Imagine where you are. What are you thinking and feeling? How is this lesson meeting you where you are and encouraging you on your journey? Color the page and add anything to make it personal.

Create

Use this page to write a prayer, thinking about where you are now and your response to Jesus asking you if you will follow him.

On the following page, create your own visual that captures what comes to your mind when you reflect on your response to Jesus asking you to follow him.

evaluate
FREEDOM
forgiveness
friendships
NEW

Reflect on what you experienced or discovered during your Empowered session when you think about each of these words.

EVALUATE

_____

_____

_____

FREEDOM

_____

_____

_____

FORGIVENESS

_____

_____

FRIENDSHIPS

_____

_____

_____

NEW

_____

_____

_____

A NOINTED WITH GOD'S BLESSING
Grace, Blessing, Peace, Identity, Value

And the One seated on the throne said, "Behold, I make all things new." Then He said, "Write this down, for these words are faithful and true." And He told me, "It is done! I am the Alpha and the Omega, the Beginning and the End. To the thirsty I will give freely from the spring of the water of life. The one who is victorious will inherit all things, and I will be his God, and he will be My son."

REVELATION 21:5-7, BSB

It is God who enables us, along with you, to stand firm for Christ. He has commissioned us, and he has identified us as his own by placing the Holy Spirit in our hearts as the first installment that guarantees everything he has promised us.

2 CORINTHIANS 1:21-22

Come, receive your identity as a daughter of God!

A time to review:

PURIFIED IN THE RIVER OF THE WATER OF LIFE.
Called, Loved, Accepted, Forgiven, Whole

EMPOWERED IN THE LIGHT OF CHRIST.
Evaluate, Freedom, Forgiveness, Friendships, New

The next part of your journey:

In this session, you will be invited to come to the River of the Water of Life that flows from the throne of God and of the Lamb to receive an anointing. It is in this place where you will discover your identity, abundant blessing, unique value, unmerited grace, and a peace that passes all understanding. You will be encouraged to grow in God's favor and faithfully live within the beautiful boundaries of his Kingdom.

Read and meditate on Revelation 21 and 22 in your Bible or on pages xxiii–xxvi. Use a purple pencil to underline every verse that has to do with being a child in the Kingdom of God.

On the picture to your right, imagine this is you coming to God.

Color the drawing, choosing colors that bring to life how you imagine this scene. Add any words or a verse from the Scripture you read.

Write the five key words for this lesson somewhere in the picture: *Grace, Blessing, Peace, Identity, Value.*

THE HOLY SPIRIT

The anointing—the oil of Scripture—is directly related to the Holy Spirit's work in your inner life.

When you make a decision to believe in Christ and follow him, the Holy Spirit enters your life. The Holy Spirit's work in you helps you in many ways.

He will *guide* you.

> He is the Holy Spirit, who leads into all truth.
> JOHN 14:17

He will *counsel* you.

> But the [Helper (Comforter, Advocate, Intercessor—Counselor, Strengthener, Standby), the Holy Spirit, whom the Father will send in My name [in My place, to represent Me and act on My behalf], He will teach you all things. And He will help you remember everything that I have told you.
> JOHN 14:26, AMP

He brings us *peace*.

> I am leaving you with a gift—peace of mind and heart. And the peace I give is a gift the world cannot give. So don't be troubled or afraid.
> JOHN 14:27

IF WE ARE TO LIVE A VICTORIOUS LIFE,

WE NEED THE TWO-SIDED GIFT GOD

HAS OFFERED US: FIRST, THE WORK OF

THE SON OF GOD FOR US; SECOND,

THE WORK OF THE SPIRIT OF GOD IN US.

We need Jesus Christ

FOR OUR ETERNAL LIFE, AND THE HOLY SPIRIT

OF GOD FOR OUR INTERNAL LIFE. THE FATHER IS

THE SOURCE OF ALL BLESSING, THE SON IS THE

CHANNEL OF ALL BLESSING, AND IT IS THROUGH

THE HOLY SPIRIT AT WORK IN US THAT ALL TRUTH

BECOMES LIVING AND OPERATIVE IN OUR LIVES.

Billy Graham

GRACE

When a single grain of sand enters the living membrane of an oyster, the oyster becomes irritated. The oyster's reaction is to continually coat it with a substance called nacre, eventually transforming the grain of sand into a beautiful pearl.

The Latin word for pearl literally means "unique," attesting to the fact that no two pearls are identical.

You and I are like those single grains of sand when we come to God. He receives us as we are, then covers us with his grace and refines us by the truth of his Word.

Through that process, he creates something beautiful in us that, each in our own unique and creative way, reflects who he is to the world around us.

Grace, by definition, is God's unmerited favor. The truth is that God accepts us as we are when we come to him. He would never say, "Oh, no, not you, you can't come. Go get yourself fixed, cleaned up, worthy, then come back." No, he says, "Come. Come just as you are."

That doesn't mean you are going to stay that way. That just means in coming to God, the only thing he asks you to do is simply come.

In what area of your life have you tried to clean yourself up before coming to God?

_____

_____

_____

_____

How have you tried to clean yourself up? Does the definition of grace—unmerited favor—shift your focus from yourself toward the One who wants to cover you in his grace? How would you describe what happens?

_____

_____

_____

_____

How do you feel after receiving God's grace?

_____

_____

_____

_____

None of us can do this alone. We need the Holy Spirit to come alongside us. Invite the Holy Spirit to come into your life as you believe in Christ. He will guide you from here as you are covered in God's grace and continue your journey of learning how to allow the truth of God's Word to transform your life.

BLESSING

I offer this blessing to you, representing the unconditional love and acceptance you receive from God your heavenly Father, and how that can transform your mind, heart, and identity.

Read these statements out loud:

- I am loved by God.
- I am accepted by God.
- I belong to God.
- I am his daughter.
- I matter to God.
- I am valuable in God's eyes.
- I have a unique, creative way to reflect God's love to others.
- I am choosing to believe what God's Word says to be true.
- He will never leave me nor forsake me. He is always with me.
- The plans he has for me are good.
- He is the same yesterday, today, and forever.
- He will guide me always.

On the page to your right, imagine you are following a path that starts from the river and winds its way up to the top of the mountain.

Write a word in each stone that helps you feel God's blessing, a word that you want to have line your path. Color the drawing and write a prayer somewhere on the page.

Create

Close your eyes and imagine you have made it to the top of the mountain where the River of the Water of Life flows from the throne of God.

God is inviting you to come to him. You kneel down before him and are surrounded by his unfailing love and endless glory light. Just as you are ready to join the angels saying, "Holy, holy, holy is the Lord God Almighty," you realize God is placing a crown upon your head.

> Holy, holy, holy is the LORD Almighty; the whole earth is full of his glory.
> ISAIAH 6:3, NIV

Imagine what it looks, feels, and sounds like as you kneel before the throne of God and of the Lamb. On the page to your right, use color and add words to reflect what you imagine.

What are you sensing God is saying to you? If something comes to you, write it on the picture somewhere.

Create

> The Spirit of the Sovereign LORD is on me, because the LORD has anointed me to preach good news to the poor. He has sent me to bind up the brokenhearted, to proclaim freedom for the captives and release from darkness for the prisoners, to proclaim the year of the LORD's favor and the day of vengeance of our God, to comfort all who mourn, and provide for those who grieve in Zion—to bestow on them a crown of beauty instead of ashes, the oil of gladness instead of mourning, and a garment of praise instead of a spirit of despair.
>
> ISAIAH 61:1-3, NIV

God covers us with his unmerited grace, adopts us as his own children, and bestows his blessing upon us. In his Kingdom, we are accepted and valued for who we are. Believing this truth takes us deeper into our transformation process.

Close your eyes and imagine being on the top of the mountain where the River of the Water of Life flows from the throne of God.

God is inviting you to come to him. You kneel down before him feeling surrounded by his unfailing love and endless glory light. Just as you are ready to join the angels saying, "Holy, holy, holy is the Lord God Almighty," you realize God is placing a crown upon your head.

Imagine what it looks like. Color the drawing to your right to reflect what your crown looks like.

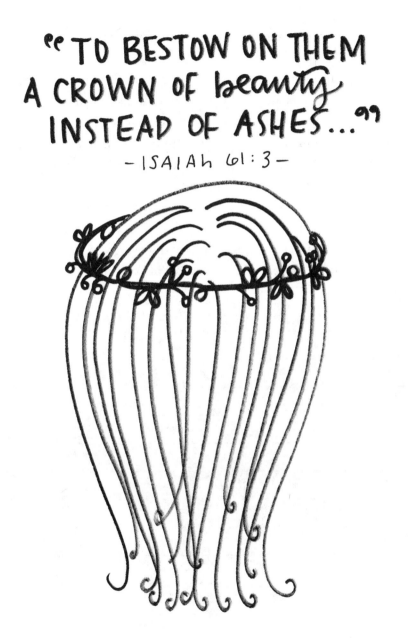

"TO BESTOW ON THEM
A CROWN OF beauty
INSTEAD OF ASHES..."

— ISAIAH 61:3 —

Create

On this page, write a prayer and/or your thoughts about what this crown means to you.

On the page to your right, color the crown and fill the space around the crown with words that share what your crown means to you.

Take some time to be still in prayer and worship before you start creating. Reflect on the Scripture and lesson. Listen in prayer. Imagine where you are. What are you thinking and feeling? How is this lesson meeting you where you are and encouraging you on your journey?

Reflect on the five key words in this session: *Grace, Blessing, Peace, Identity, Value.*

As you think about everything you have discovered so far, how can these words bring meaning to your life and be part of your crown?

_____

_____

_____

_____

_____

_____

_____

_____

_____

_____

_____

crown
OF BEAUTY

PEACE

MAY THE LORD BLESS YOU

and protect you.

MAY THE LORD SMILE ON YOU

and be gracious to you.

MAY THE LORD SHOW YOU HIS FAVOR AND

give you his peace.

Numbers 6:24-26

On the page to your right, color the drawing in a way that reflects the peace in your spirit now that you have received God's blessing over your life.

Write three words, one on each of the mountains, that describe how the peace of God has settled over you after receiving your crown.

Add anything else to the picture that comes to your mind.

IDENTITY

In this session, you will dig deeper into the meaning of your name. To the people of Israel, a name was more than an identification tag. Names had deep significance and were chosen carefully to have meaning and purpose.

As you have come to the River of the Water of Life, you have experienced transformation and are beginning to understand more deeply who you truly are now that you are free from your past and listening to the truth of God's holy Word over your life.

In prayer, begin to explore what your name means after all you have learned and discovered on your journey so far.

> *Dear God,*
>   *With all that you have done in my life up to this point, can*
>   *you help me bring spiritual significance to my name?*

See an example of how this is done on the page to your right.

Then on the spread that follows:

On the left side of the spread write a prayer or journal your thoughts, telling the story of why you are choosing the words for each letter of your name.

On the right side of the spread, write you own name like you see in the example on your right here. Choose words that reflect who you are in Christ with your new identity.

M - MADE whole

A - ANOINTED

D - DAUGHTER OF GOD

I - INSPIRED

S - SET free

O - ONE·OF·A·KIND

N - NEW CREATION

On this page, write a prayer or journal your thoughts. On the page to your right, create the meaning of your name.

_____

_____

_____

_____

_____

_____

_____

_____

_____

_____

_____

_____

_____

_____

_____

_____

_____

_____

_____

_____

_____

_____

_____

A NOTE FROM GOD TO YOU

To my daughter _____,

I have something special that I would like to give you. It is something I want to make sure you know and, more importantly, believe.

Close your eyes.

Come to the River of the Water of Life that flows from my throne where the glory of Christ shines down upon you.

You are now standing before me. I place in your hand a legal piece of paper rolled up into a scroll tied with a beautiful blue ribbon. Untie the ribbon, open the scroll, and read the words. They are very important words.

I am your Father. You are my daughter. You are now in my family. Everything I have is yours. When you need something to fulfill the vision I have given you, all you have to do is ask me. You are not alone. I am with you! On the page to your right, color the drawing to reflect how you feel, adding any words or a prayer.

Grace
BLESSING
PEACE
IDENTITY
VALUE

Reflect on what you experienced or discovered during your Anointed session when you think about each of these words.

GRACE

_____

_____

_____

BLESSING

_____

_____

_____

PEACE

_____

_____

_____

IDENTITY

_____

_____

_____

VALUE

_____

_____

_____

R OOTED IN GOD'S PERFECT LOVE
Truth, Nourished, Healthy, Strong, Confident

When I think of all this, I fall to my knees and pray to the Father, the Creator of everything in heaven and on earth. I pray that from his glorious, unlimited resources he will empower you with inner strength through his Spirit. Then Christ will make his home in your hearts as you trust in him. Your roots will grow down into God's love and keep you strong. And may you have the power to understand, as all God's people should, how wide, how long, how high, and how deep his love is. May you experience the love of Christ, though it is too great to understand fully. Then you will be made complete with all the fullness of life and power that comes from God.

EPHESIANS 3:14-19

Being rooted in the truth of God's love for you will help you stand firm and be nourished with everything you need in order to be filled with all the fullness of God.

A time to review:

PURIFIED IN THE RIVER OF THE WATER OF LIFE.
Called, Loved, Accepted, Forgiven, Whole.

EMPOWERED IN THE LIGHT OF CHRIST.
Evaluate, Freedom, Forgiveness, Friendships, New.

ANOINTED WITH GOD'S BLESSING.
Grace, Blessing, Peace, Identity, Value.

The next part of your journey:

In this session, you will be invited to come to the River of the Water of Life that flows from the throne of God and of the Lamb, and be Rooted and grounded in God's love for you.

Read and meditate on Revelation 22:1 in your Bible or on page xxv, and Ephesians 3:14-19 in your Bible or on page 99. Use a green pencil to underline every verse that has to do with being a tree of God's love.

On the picture to your right, imagine you are coming to the river to plant your life like a tree, with roots going down deep into the soil of God's marvelous love.

Color the drawing, choosing colors that bring to life how you imagine this scene. Add any words that come to your mind or from the Scripture you just read.

Write the five key words for this lesson somewhere in the picture: *Truth, Nourished, Healthy, Strong, Confident.*

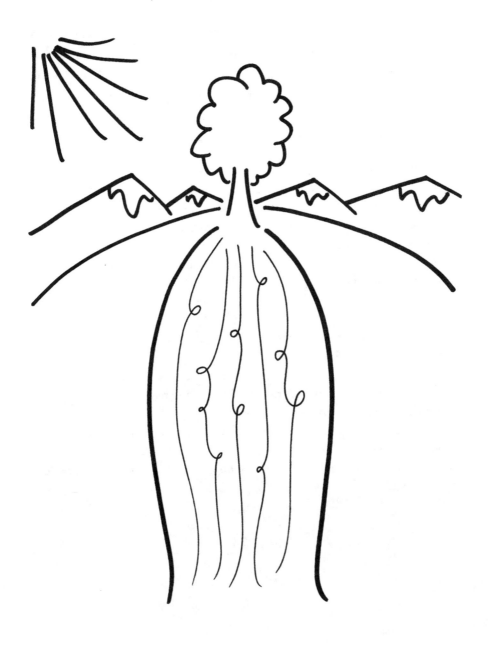

When I first started my own journey of discovering God's love, it took some time to wrap my mind around the truth that God loves me unconditionally. The more I explored what the Bible helps us know about God and his love, the more I opened my heart to him and began to experience how his love can flow into my life here on earth.

Let's begin to explore what God's love is like as described in 1 Corinthians 13:

If I could speak all the languages of earth and of angels, but didn't love others, I would only be a noisy gong or a clanging cymbal. If I had the gift of prophecy, and if I understood all of God's secret plans and possessed all knowledge, and if I had such faith that I could move mountains, but didn't love others, I would be nothing. If I gave everything I have to the poor and even sacrificed my body, I could boast about it; but if I didn't love others, I would have gained nothing.

Love is patient and kind. Love is not jealous or boastful or proud or rude. It does not demand its own way. It is not irritable, and it keeps no record of being wronged. It does not rejoice about injustice but rejoices whenever the truth wins out. Love never gives up, never loses faith, is always hopeful, and endures through every circumstance.

. . . Now we see things imperfectly, like puzzling reflections in a mirror, but then we will see everything with perfect clarity. All that I know now is partial and incomplete, but then I will know everything completely, just as God now knows me completely.

Three things will last forever—faith, hope, and love—and the greatest of these is love.

GOD IS LOVE

Let's start taking a closer look at each of the manifestations of God's love.

- Love is patient.
- Love is kind.
- Love is content (does not envy).
- Love is humble (not boastful or arrogant).
- Love is respectful (not rude).
- Love values others (not insisting on its own way).
- Love is peaceful (not irritable).
- Love is forgiving (not resentful).
- Love is pure (does not rejoice in wrongdoings).
- Love is truthful.
- Love is protecting.
- Love is trusting.
- Love is hopeful.
- Love is persevering.

God is love.

1 JOHN 4:8

SUCH LOVE HAS NO FEAR, BECAUSE

perfect love expels all fear.

IF WE ARE AFRAID, IT IS FOR FEAR OF PUNISHMENT,

AND THIS SHOWS THAT WE HAVE NOT FULLY

EXPERIENCED HIS PERFECT LOVE.

WE LOVE EACH OTHER BECAUSE

he loved us first.

1 John 4:18-19

Create

On the following page:

Imagine what it would look like if you were a tree planted by the river that flows from the throne of God, and your roots went down deep into the soil and waters of God's love. The tree by the river will become a symbol of you being rooted like a tree in the love of God.

Reflect on everything you have read about God's love so far.

Write words in the water that describe God's love.

Somewhere on the page, write words that describe how you have experienced God's love in your life.

Color the picture to reflect how you feel.

At the River of the Water of Life that flows from the throne of God and of the Lamb, you learn how to put your roots down deep into God's love. Being rooted in the truth of God's love for you will help you stand firm and be nourished with everything you need to be filled with all the fullness of God.

In Ephesians 3:14-19, Scripture tells us to put our roots down deep into God's love.

> When I think of all this, I fall to my knees and pray to the Father, the Creator of everything in heaven and on earth. I pray that from his glorious, unlimited resources he will empower you with inner strength through his Spirit. Then Christ will make his home in your hearts as you trust in him. Your roots will grow down into God's love and keep you strong. And may you have the power to understand, as all God's people should, how wide, how long, how high, and how deep his love is. May you experience the love of Christ, though it is too great to understand fully. Then you will be made complete with all the fullness of life and power that comes from God.
>
> EPHESIANS 3:14-19

AN HONEST EVALUATION

It's time to honestly evaluate the condition of your current roots and assess your desire to make some changes going forward.

Circle the words in the left column that may define a root you currently have that you want to pull up and circle the words in the right column that you would like to put down. Add additional words that come to you in the lines below.

Use words to summarize
the roots you are **pulling up**.

Examples:

Pride
Envy
Resentment
Anger
Bitterness
Selfishness
Fear
Rejection
Shame
Hate
Manipulation
Critical spirit
Controlling
Lies

Use words to summarize
the roots you are **putting down**.

Examples:

Patient
Kind
Humble
Forgiving
Truthful
Valued
Respectful
Protecting
Hopeful
Persevering
Pure
Peaceful
Accepted
Belonging

_____

_____

_____

Now that you know what you want your roots to look and feel like, let's start your process of getting there. On the following pages, you will write your own prayer; the prayer on this page is an example to help you get started.

Dear God,

Thank you for your love. Thank you that you love me! I want to be like a tree, planted by the river that flows from your throne. I desire for my roots to be established only in your perfect love.

In looking at all the pieces of my life, I ask that you come and help me to know how to remove roots that are blocking your love and hurting my life.

Spiritually, I ask that you remove all roots from my life that are not grounded in the lordship and authority of Jesus Christ. This includes past generational sins and curses and anything in the present that I have brought into my life.

Mentally, I ask that you help me remove all roots that are based on lies, such as mental tapes that tell me I am not good enough, not smart enough, not pretty enough, not valued.

Emotionally, I ask that you help me remove all roots that are based on past experiences, such as rejection, abandonment, fear, anxiety, bitterness, anger, hurt.

Relationally, help me to disconnect from relationships and create healthy boundaries so other people cannot poison my root system any longer.

Physically, help me be careful to put into my body only what will bring nourishment and health.

Create

Write your prayer on the lines below, adding a prayer over each of the five parts of your life—spiritually, mentally, emotionally, physically, and relationally.

_____

_____

_____

_____

_____

_____

_____

_____

_____

_____

_____

_____

_____

_____

_____

_____

_____

_____

_____

PULLING UP

Now that you know what you want your roots to look and feel like, let's start your process of getting there. God desires that you be filled with his fullness. In order for this to happen, it's good to make sure nothing is blocking the Water of the River of Life from flowing through your roots into every part of your life.

A Christian counselor can help.
If you feel overwhelmed with this process, find a skilled Christian counselor to help coach you through this process. But if you feel like you can do this with the Holy Spirit by your side, continue on.

Consider tools for your journey.
These are tools you can use to help you on your own personal journey of pulling up roots.

Grab a separate notebook.
In this next session, you will use a separate notebook to process pulling up your roots.

Identify which roots you need to pull up.
In your separate notebook, write down all the words that represent a root you want to pull up out of your life. I wish it were as simple as making a list of all the unhealthy roots and tossing them into the trash, but it is not. Making a list is an important part of the process so you can identify what you are working with.

Create a new page for each root you want to pull up.
In your notebook, make a separate page for each root you want to pull up.

Proceed one root at a time.
This is something that takes time. I suggest focusing on one root at a time.

Consider "rejection" as an example.
We will use the example of "rejection" as an unhealthy root for coaching in the pages to come.

Start writing.
This is for your eyes only since this is a private journey to help you process. Start with the first root you want to pull up out of your life and keep doing this with others over time. For example, say a root you want to pull up is rejection. One of the best steps to help you get something out of your mind and heart is to "get it out" by writing or drawing or using some other form to help you process your thoughts and emotions. Start writing about how this root got there.

What do you want to say?
Get everything out that is pent up inside of your mind or heart. What caused this root to get in the picture of your life? Continue writing until you have said everything you want to say. Remember, this is for your eyes only.

What steps can you take to change?
What steps can you start taking today that will help you get closer to what you want your tree to look like?

TAKE IT TO THE RIVER

With your words in your hand, close your eyes and visualize yourself coming to the river to talk to God about all that you just wrote.

In prayer, be still and talk to God and let him talk to you. During this process, he may ask you questions. Take time to listen for his voice and have conversations with him about everything you are feeling.

On the following page, write your own prayer, similar to this example:

> *Dear God,*
>
> *I come before you and ask that your Holy Spirit would help me reach even deeper than I could myself and pull this root of rejection out of my life for good. I invite you, Holy Spirit, in the name of Jesus Christ, to look deep inside of me and make sure this root is pulled out completely.*
>
> *I now hold this root in my hand, and I choose to toss it into the river where all the negative energy that was taking up space in my life is purified in the waters of your perfect love.*
>
> *Where I once was clogged from life, I ask that you pour your love and acceptance into my life and create in me a new root based only on your love, which brings life.*

Write your own prayer on the lines below.

_____

_____

_____

_____

_____

_____

_____

_____

_____

_____

_____

_____

_____

_____

_____

_____

_____

_____

_____

_____

_____

_____

Let Go

Write down everything you want to let go of on this page.

On the page to your right, write your words into the picture to symbolize how you are letting them go. Include a prayer.

_____

_____

_____

_____

_____

_____

_____

_____

_____

_____

_____

_____

_____

_____

_____

_____

_____

_____

_____

_____

_____

_____

_____

_____

_____

Receive

Write down everything you want to receive from God on this page.

On the page to your right, write your words into the picture to symbolize how you are receiving those gifts from God. Include a prayer.

_____

_____

_____

_____

_____

_____

_____

_____

_____

_____

_____

_____

_____

_____

_____

_____

_____

_____

_____

_____

_____

_____

_____

HEALTHY ROOTS

Both the Old and New Testaments teach us valuable lessons from the plant world. The prophet Jeremiah used the analogy of a person filled with faith as being like a strong, flourishing tree.

> Blessed are those who trust in the LORD and have made the LORD their hope and confidence. They are like trees planted along a riverbank, with roots that reach deep into the water. Such trees are not bothered by the heat or worried by long months of drought. Their leaves stay green, and they never stop producing fruit.
>
> JEREMIAH 17:7-8

Reflect on everything you have learned so far in this session. You have let go of unhealthy roots. You have received God's love into your life in new ways.

On the page to your right, use this drawing to help you create a visual reminder of what your goal is, as you think about being a tree with healthy roots planted in the water of God's love.

Imagine your tree is planted in the river of God's love. What would you name each of your roots? Write a name on each root.

Be encouraged as you see your life through God's eyes and create healthy roots, so all the pieces of who you are have a clear path for nourishment to flow through.

Create

On the following page, draw your own picture, write a prayer, or illustrate what you feel now and about what you want going forward in your life from this place.

Here is an example prayer:

> *Dear God, my Father,*
>
> *From this day forward, I will come to you at the River of the Water of Life for everything I need to have a healthy tree. I come to you for acceptance, unconditional love, belonging, value, protection, purpose, and life.*
>
> *I thank you for all the people who are in my life. I will no longer let anyone tangle me up in their roots. Instead, I will make sure I keep space around myself so I can breathe and will make sure my roots are going down deep into your love.*
>
> *I will also make sure I do not stretch my roots into other people's spaces, but I will get what I need from you. I will be responsible with the energy I bring to each space and will honor other people who cross my path.*
>
> *I pray you will continue to bring community into my life where we all can grow together and share life together in healthy ways and learn to love each other from our own wells of life coming from you. Thank you for your unfailing love!*

Reflect on what you experienced or discovered during your Rooted session as you think about each of these words.

TRUTH

_____

_____

_____

NOURISHED

_____

_____

_____

HEALTHY

_____

_____

_____

STRONG

_____

_____

_____

CONFIDENT

_____

_____

_____

LIVING TO REFLECT GOD'S LOVE IN YOUR OWN UNIQUE WAY
Dream, Explore, Discover, Purpose, Create

Then the angel showed me THE RIVER of the water of life, bright as crystal, flowing from the throne of God and of the Lamb through the middle of the street of the city; also, on either side of the river, THE TREE OF LIFE with its twelve kinds of fruit, yielding its fruit each month. The LEAVES of the tree were for the HEALING of the nations.

REVELATION 22:1-2, ESV (EMPHASIS ADDED)

Come to Jesus and be filled with Life, so you can reflect him beautifully and uniquely to the world around you.

A time to review:

PURIFIED IN THE RIVER OF THE WATER OF LIFE.
Called, Loved, Accepted, Forgiven, Whole.

EMPOWERED IN THE LIGHT OF CHRIST.
Evaluate, Freedom, Forgiveness, Friendships, New.

ANOINTED WITH GOD'S BLESSING.
Grace, Blessing, Peace, Identity, Value.

ROOTED IN GOD'S PERFECT LOVE.
Truth, Nourished, Healthy, Strong, Confident.

The next part of your journey:

In this session, you are going to explore how being filled with the Life of Christ can create leaves on your tree that bring healing, love, and life to others.

Read and meditate on Revelation 21 and 22 in your Bible or on pages xxiii–xxvi. Use a green pencil to underline every verse that has to do with your tree and life.

On the picture to your right, imagine this is the tree of your life.

Color the drawing, choosing colors that bring to life how you imagine this scene. Add any words or a verse from the Scripture you read.

Write the five key words for this lesson somewhere in the picture: *Dream, Explore, Discover, Purpose, Create.*

Reflect on the meaning of your pearl.

When a single grain of sand enters the living membrane of an oyster, the oyster becomes irritated. The oyster's reaction is to continually coat it with a substance called nacre, eventually transforming the grain of sand into a beautiful pearl.

The Latin word for pearl literally means "unique," attesting to the fact that no two pearls are identical.

You and I are like those single grains of sand when we come to God. He receives us as we are, then covers us with his grace, and refines us by the truth of his Word.

Through that process, he creates something beautiful in us that, each in our own unique and creative way, reflects who he is to the world around us.

Reflect on your journey so far.

In Purified, you were invited to come to the River of the Water of Life and make a connection with God through his Son, Jesus Christ. You were accepted as you are and began your creative journey of transformation.

In Empowered, you invited Jesus, the Light of the World, to shine into all areas of your life and set you free from the chains that were holding you back.

In Anointed, you came before God your Father to receive your identity as a daughter of God. You received God's blessing over your life, your crown, and a new name.

In Rooted, you established your roots deep into God's love to grow as a daughter of God in his Kingdom.

In Life (this session), you will allow the life that flows from God's love to bring nutrients to your tree. This will produce leaves and fruit on your tree that will bring hope and healing to others.

It is through this entire process of your journey that Jesus is cultivating your pearl, as he creates something beautiful in you, in your own unique and creative way, that reflects who he is to the world around you.

A TREE OF LIFE

Then the angel showed me the river of the water of life, bright as crystal, flowing from the throne of God and of the Lamb through the middle of the street of the city; also, on either side of the river, the tree of life with its twelve kinds of fruit, yielding its fruit each month. The leaves of the tree were for the healing of the nations.

No longer will there be anything accursed, but the throne of God and of the Lamb will be in it, and his servants will worship him. They will see his face, and his name will be on their foreheads. And night will be no more. They will need no light of lamp or sun, for the Lord God will be their light, and they will reign forever and ever.

REVELATION 22:1-5, ESV

On the following page, draw a picture of what you imagine after reading this Scripture and reflecting on your journey so far. Review the last couple of pages as well. Consider your next step of the journey: becoming a tree of life.

Include a prayer to God, asking what you desire from him as you begin your process of being filled with life.

ABIDE IN CHRIST

The Bible describes the fruit on your tree as being cultivated by abiding in Christ and allowing the Holy Spirit to work in your life.

> Remain in me, and I will remain in you. For a branch cannot produce fruit if it is severed from the vine, and you cannot be fruitful unless you remain in me. Yes, I am the vine; you are the branches. Those who remain in me, and I in them, will produce much fruit. For apart from me you can do nothing.
>
> JOHN 15:4-5

> The Holy Spirit produces this kind of fruit in our lives: love, joy, peace, patience, kindness, goodness, faithfulness, gentleness, and self-control. There is no law against these things!
>
> GALATIANS 5:22-23

On the following page:

Illustrate what it would look like if you were a tree planted by the river that flows from the throne of God.

First, name your roots that you worked on in the last session. Then start to add fruit to your tree.

Take a good look at the root words and the fruit words. Do you see any correlations? If so, what did you discover? Add leaves that are meant to bring healing to the nations. What words would you use to describe the leaves on your tree?

HEALING LEAVES

When you have been purified, empowered, anointed, rooted, and filled with life, you are now able to fulfill your purpose while on this earth.

How you creatively reflect what you have allowed the Holy Spirit to do in you will become the leaves of your tree that will bring healing and hope to others.

The leaves are a symbol of how your life will make an impact on others and bring God's love to them wherever they are on their own journey.

Whether you become a

- Writer
- Photographer
- Artist
- Scientist
- Doctor
- Lawyer
- Athlete
- Banker
- Accountant
- Whatever you decide to be . . .

You bring God's love and the beauty of his Kingdom with you wherever you go.

Color in the picture to your right.

A TIME TO EXPLORE

On the following pages, we are going to spend time helping you cultivate the leaves on your tree. You'll be thinking about dreams you have in your heart, passions you want to pursue, and gifts you have been entrusted with.

MAKE A CAREFUL EXPLORATION OF

who you are.

DON'T BE IMPRESSED WITH YOURSELF. . . .

DON'T COMPARE YOURSELF WITH OTHERS.

EACH OF YOU MUST TAKE RESPONSIBILITY FOR

doing the creative best

YOU CAN WITH YOUR OWN LIFE.

Galatians 6:4-5, MSG

On the page to your right, draw something that comes to your mind when reflecting on this verse and that also expresses who you are.

Unique Qualities

What are five qualities about yourself that make you unique? Write your five words on the lines below, elaborating on each one.

_____

_____

_____

_____

_____

_____

_____

_____

_____

_____

_____

_____

_____

_____

_____

_____

_____

_____

_____

_____

Favorite Things

What are your favorite things to do in your free time?

_____

_____

_____

_____

_____

_____

_____

_____

_____

_____

_____

_____

_____

_____

_____

_____

_____

_____

_____

_____

_____

_____

Lessons from Nature

All the Beauty to be found throughout the whole creation is but a reflection of the diffused beams of that being who has fullness of brightness and glory . . . GOD.

JONATHAN EDWARDS, AMERICAN THEOLOGIAN

What lessons have you learned from nature?

_____

_____

_____

_____

_____

_____

_____

_____

_____

_____

_____

_____

_____

_____

_____

_____

_____

Overcoming Adversity

What lessons have you learned from overcoming adversity?

_____

_____

_____

_____

_____

_____

_____

_____

_____

_____

_____

_____

_____

_____

_____

_____

_____

_____

_____

_____

Life-Shaping Experiences

What are five lessons you have learned from your experiences that have shaped your life?

_____

_____

_____

_____

_____

_____

_____

_____

_____

_____

_____

_____

_____

_____

_____

_____

_____

_____

_____

_____

_____

Pearls and Diamonds

We refer to Pearls (women) and Diamonds (men) as people who have positively impacted our life and added value to it. Think about family members, teachers, role models, and mentors who have done that for you. It can even be someone you have never met in person, but their life somehow impacted yours.

Write the names of your Pearls and Diamonds and share how each one has added value to your life.

_____

_____

_____

_____

_____

_____

_____

_____

_____

_____

_____

_____

_____

_____

_____

_____

_____

Your Strengths

What are your strengths? List every one you can think of and why you consider them strengths.

_____

_____

_____

_____

_____

_____

_____

_____

_____

_____

_____

_____

_____

_____

_____

_____

_____

_____

_____

_____

Bring Joy

What is something you like to do that brings joy to others? Why?

_____

_____

_____

_____

_____

_____

_____

_____

_____

_____

_____

_____

_____

_____

_____

_____

_____

_____

_____

Dream

What dream do you have in your mind and heart that you would like to achieve this year? In the next five years? In your lifetime? Take some time to write something for each time line.

_____

_____

_____

_____

_____

_____

_____

_____

_____

_____

_____

_____

_____

_____

_____

_____

_____

_____

_____

_____

Be a Pearl

If you were a "big sister" to a younger girl for a day, where would you take her and what would you do? Why? Who can you be a pearl to? How can you start now?

_____

_____

_____

_____

_____

_____

_____

_____

_____

_____

_____

_____

_____

_____

_____

_____

_____

_____

_____

Words of Life

Imagine you have been asked to share at an upcoming conference for girls. You can choose a breakout session focused on any range of ages. What age group would you choose? What would you want to share with them?

_____

_____

_____

_____

_____

_____

_____

_____

_____

_____

_____

_____

_____

_____

_____

_____

_____

_____

_____

_____

_____

Make a Difference

As you look over your life up to this point, staying in the flow of your unique story, how would you like to make a difference in the life of another girl or other girls? Imagine you have one day to do something special. What would you do? How can you make this a reality and actually do it?

_____

_____

_____

_____

_____

_____

_____

_____

_____

_____

_____

_____

_____

_____

_____

_____

_____

_____

In His Presence

Throughout history and continuing to today, the girls and women who are making an impact for Kingdom purposes all have one thing in common—they spend time with God in his presence and come out of that place reflecting something beautiful to the world around them.

On this page, reflect on everything you have explored in this session so far. Take some time to bring it all to God in prayer. Meditate on how you can reflect God's love to the world in a way that flows from your life and experiences and gifts. These insights will become the leaves on your tree.

How have you allowed the study and application of God's Word to transform your life?

_____

_____

_____

_____

How have you allowed the grace of God to shape your life? How will you continue this going forward?

_____

_____

_____

_____

_____

_____

_____

_____

_____

My Life Words

Choose four words that you want to define your life, thinking of them as the four corners of your land.

For example: Freedom, Peace, Blessing, Beauty.

1. _____

2. _____

3. _____

4. _____

Choose twelve words that you want to become the foundation of your life.

For example: Love, Pure, Empowered, Rooted, Anointed, Life, Release, Reflect, Truth, Inspire, Create, Heal.

1. _____

2. _____

3. _____

4. _____

5. _____

6. _____

7. _____

8. _____

9. _____

10. _____

11. _____

12. _____

Scripture Verses That Guide Me

Write down three Scripture verses that encourage you and that flow from everything you have been reflecting on. How are they a light to your path? Write out the entire verses, not just the references.

_____

_____

_____

_____

_____

_____

_____

_____

_____

_____

_____

_____

_____

_____

_____

_____

_____

_____

_____

_____

THE LEAVES OF YOUR TREE

On the following spread, think about everything you have been writing about and create a visual representation of the leaves on your tree.

Try to bring many of the pieces you have written about into your drawing or visual representation. Flip back through the pages of this section to gather ideas.

Take some time to be still in prayer and consider what you would name your leaves.

Reflect on these verses:

Then the angel showed me the river of the water of life, bright as crystal, flowing from the throne of God and of the Lamb through the middle of the street of the city; also, on either side of the river, the tree of life with its twelve kinds of fruit, yielding its fruit each month. The leaves of the tree were for the healing of the nations.

REVELATION 22:1-2

In your visual representation include:

Drawing,
Words,
Color,
Scripture,
And whatever else comes to you mind.
Date the page.

WRITE YOUR THOUGHTS AND IDEAS

_____

_____

_____

_____

_____

_____

_____

_____

_____

_____

_____

_____

_____

_____

_____

_____

_____

_____

_____

_____

_____

_____

_____

_____

_____

_____

Create your
visual picture.

DREAM
EXPLORE
discover
purpose
CREATE

Reflect on what you experienced or discovered during your Life session as you think about each of these words.

DREAM

_____

_____

_____

EXPLORE

_____

_____

_____

DISCOVER

_____

_____

_____

PURPOSE

_____

_____

_____

CREATE

_____

_____

_____

Sacred Covenant

MAKE IT BEAUTIFUL!

For we are God's masterpiece. He has created us anew in Christ Jesus, so we can do the good things he planned for us long ago.

EPHESIANS 2:10

Anyone who believes in me may come and drink! For the Scriptures declare, "Rivers of living water will flow from his heart."

JOHN 7:38

Now it is your turn to consider how the leaves of your tree can become a blessing to others.

A time to review:

PURIFIED IN THE RIVER OF THE WATER OF LIFE.
Called, Loved, Accepted, Forgiven, Whole.

EMPOWERED IN THE LIGHT OF CHRIST.
Evaluate, Freedom, Forgiveness, Friendships, New.

ANOINTED WITH GOD'S BLESSING.
Grace, Blessing, Peace, Identity, Value.

ROOTED IN GOD'S PERFECT LOVE.
Truth, Nourished, Healthy, Strong, Confident.

LIVING TO REFLECT GOD'S LOVE IN YOUR OWN UNIQUE WAY.
Dream, Explore, Discover, Purpose, Create.

The next part of your journey:

In this session, you are going to explore the idea of making a covenant with God. This will become a very meaningful and beautiful way to continue your journey from here. First, we will review the vision for this book and the journey you have been on.

When the vision for this book first came to me, I was in prayer. You may remember reading this at the beginning of your journey, but I want to review this part of the vision, as it is important for where you are right now.

I had been reading Revelation 21 and 22 and imagining what the words were communicating to me.

The Scripture painted a picture of this beautiful river that flows from the throne of God, and I imagined Jesus in this river calling me to come to him.

As I kept this picture in my mind, I found myself imagining that Jesus was reaching for something deep down in the water. I could see golden light and beautiful blue water slightly moving as he brought his hand up to the surface.

I was curious and found myself asking him in prayer, "Jesus, what are you doing?"

Now his eyes were fixed on me, and his light and glory flowed all over me as his simple answer found its way deep into my spirit.

"I'm cultivating pearls," he said, as his hand broke the surface of the water, revealing one of his treasures.

He held a solitary pearl before me and said, "This is Saylor. This is her story and how she is letting me transform her life, just like you did." He reached for another. "This is Courtney." And another. "This is Morgan."

Over and over, he showed me girls from all over the world. Each one trusted him with her life and placed herself in his Living Water.

It is the most beautiful scene. Jesus told me each girl's story, of what she had been through. He showed me how he was covering each one of them with his grace and shaping her by the truth of his Word. The girls were like trees—firmly rooted and growing in faith and love. As each one flourished, I saw her leaves blowing off her tree and bringing hope and healing to others.

I sensed Jesus asking me to write a book that would teach girls how to go on a creative journey of transformation and pass on many of the lessons that have helped me in my own life.

I humbly knelt before the River of the Water of Life and slipped my hands into the water as a symbol of my dedication to fulfill the assignment he was asking me to undertake.

"What is the most important thing?" I asked.

"Make It Beautiful!" he answered.

A PURE KINGDOM

[JESUS SAYS,]

"ANYONE WHO BELIEVES IN ME

MAY COME AND DRINK!

FOR THE SCRIPTURES DECLARE,

'Rivers of living water

WILL FLOW FROM HIS HEART.'"

John 7:38

On the following pages take some time to reflect on the Kingdom of God and how you feel this relates to your own life and heart. God does not ask us to live perfect lives, but he does ask us to live pure lives. There is a big difference between a perfect life and a pure one, and it is worth considering how you think about this.

Consider how you can join God in bringing love and life to others.

See the example to your right of what you will create after you answer the questions on the following pages.

Open your Bible to Revelation 21 and 22 for the next few pages. If you don't have a Bible, you can read these verses on pages xxiii–xxvi.

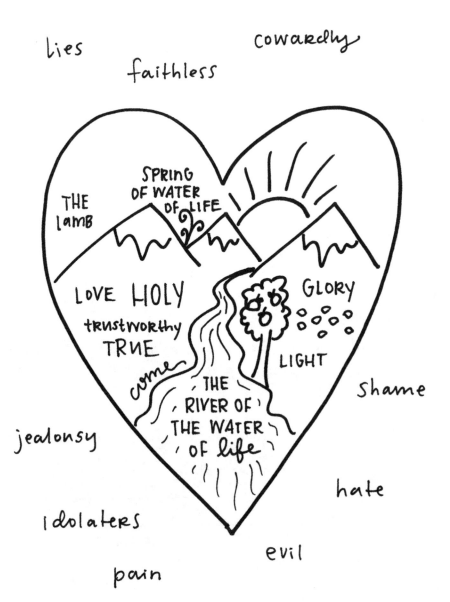

Reflect on Revelation 21 and 22 to find your answers to the following questions.

Where is God in the Kingdom?

_____

_____

_____

What is happening around the throne?

_____

_____

_____

Choose five words to describe what is happening around the throne of God and of the Lamb.

_____

_____

_____

If the Kingdom of God is _in_ your heart, where is God in your heart?

_____

_____

_____

A PURE HEART

As you visualize that through your belief in Christ your heart is the home of the Kingdom of God while you are on earth, imagine the lines of your heart are the Kingdom boundary lines. Write down all the words you can think of that you would like to reflect what is going on inside your heart. As you consider what words to choose, reflect on the Scripture passages that help us know what the Kingdom of God is like.

_____

_____

_____

_____

_____

_____

_____

_____

_____

_____

_____

_____

_____

_____

_____

_____

Create

Create a visual with words and drawing to reflect what you want to keep *outside* of your heart.

Create

Create your own heart picture with words to reflect what you would like to cultivate *inside* your heart.

A PROMISE

Reflect on everything you have discovered on your journey so far. In prayer, imagine yourself coming to Jesus at the River of the Water of Life. Ask Jesus how you can join him in bringing his love to the world around you in a beautiful way. It doesn't have to be something big. In fact, it's a good idea to start with something manageable that you feel confident you can faithfully complete.

What is Jesus asking you to do?

_____

_____

_____

What are you asking Jesus to do?

_____

_____

_____

The page to your right:

As a symbol of placing your hands in the water as I did, consider symbolically placing your pearl in the river as seen in the picture to your right. Somewhere on the page write down what you feel like Jesus is asking you to do. Color the drawing.

The next four pages:

On the following four pages you will have room to process your commitment with words, prayer, and by creating a visual representation of your own Sacred Covenant.

Use drawing, words, prayer, and Scripture. Date the pages.

And the one sitting on the throne said, "Look, I am making everything new!" And then he said to me, "Write this down, for what I tell you is trustworthy and true."

And he also said, "It is finished! I am the Alpha and the Omega—the Beginning and the End. To all who are thirsty I will give freely from the springs of the water of life.

All who are victorious will inherit all these blessings, and I will be their God, and they will be my children.

REVELATION 21:5-7

Write a prayer.

MAKE IT BEAUTIFUL

My hope for you is that you will not only know about the Kingdom of God, but that the beauty of the Kingdom of God will become the very center of your heart, flow into all the pieces of your life, and eventually flow out of your life to bring blessing to others in a beautiful way that is unique to you.

Create a visual representation of what you feel Jesus is asking you to do, in order to bring love and life to others through a sacred covenant. How can you do this in the most beautiful way you can imagine?

A PRAYER FOR YOU

This prayer is for _____ (write your name.)

In your willingness to process throughout the pages of this book, I ask our Father to complete each of the processes in your spirit, mind, heart, relationships, and body. That you will be beautifully purified, empowered, anointed, rooted, and filled with the life of Christ.

I pray you will be purified in the River of the Water of Life. That when you come to him and enter into the waters that flow from his throne, you will be overcome by his unconditional love and feel accepted, pure, and restored.

I pray that you will be empowered in the Light of Christ. That as you take time to evaluate your life, you will be set completely free from anything that holds you in chains, and you will be set free to be who God created you to be.

I pray that you will receive the anointing of God's blessing upon your head. That as he covers you with his favor, grace, honor, and glory, you will truly see yourself as he sees you. As you see yourself with a crown on your head and a new name, you will believe that you matter to God. You will know you have been chosen, adopted, and set apart as his daughter.

I pray that you will be rooted deeply into the soil of God's love for your life. That the truth of God's love and all the manifestations of his love will be free to flow up through your roots into every part of who you are. And that you will feel settled in this place of abiding in Christ. Whatever you are searching for or feel you need, you will know you will not find it in another person, another location, or another relationship. You will only find it in Christ. I pray that you keep your roots going down deep and deeper still, until you find what you need.

I pray that you will be filled with life and set apart as a carrier of his presence to shine in a unique and creative way to the world around you. I pray that you will reflect him beautifully! And that the nations will know and believe that he is faithful and true!

As you talk to God about the dreams and assignments he has for you, remember the promises of his Word that he will always be with you. Whatever you need at any point along your journey, make sure to have that honest talk with him about your thoughts and feelings.

In your honesty, remember that he is holy. Bring your honesty to him in a way that respects the holiness of the ground you are walking on.

As you continue your journey, I pray you keep the Kingdom of God at the center of your heart, and that this beauty will flow into all the parts of your life.

I pray that the ears of your spirit will always hear the voice of God whisper to you, calling out continually, "'Come.' Let anyone who hears this say, 'Come.' Let anyone who is thirsty come. Let anyone who desires drink freely from the water of life" (Revelation 22:17).

A time to review:

I'm proud of you for being consistent on your *Cultivating Pearls* creative journey of transformation! Look at all you have experienced!

PURIFIED IN THE RIVER OF THE WATER OF LIFE.
Called, Loved, Accepted, Forgiven, Whole.

EMPOWERED IN THE LIGHT OF CHRIST.
Evaluate, Freedom, Forgiveness, Friendships, New.

ANOINTED WITH GOD'S BLESSING.
Grace, Blessing, Peace, Identity, Value.

ROOTED IN GOD'S PERFECT LOVE.
Truth, Nourished, Healthy, Strong, Confident.

LIVING TO REFLECT GOD'S LOVE IN YOUR OWN UNIQUE WAY.
Dream, Explore, Discover, Purpose, Create.

SACRED COVENANT.
Make it Beautiful!

As you go from here . . .

abide IN CHRIST
KEEP IT ORGANIC
HAVE FAITH
STAY UNIQUE
BE CREATIVE
WORK HARD
BE patient
HAVE COURAGE
BE faithful
MAKE IT *beautiful*

REFLECT ON YOUR ENTIRE JOURNEY

The Greek word *teleios* is derived from the word meaning to "bring to completion" or "perfect" or "complete" or "to bring to fulfillment" the vision God has for your life. Like a pearl, there is a process we go through before the pearl is mature and can be harvested, arriving at the point where it can reflect the beauty of what went on "in the oyster" for the time it was being transformed.

It takes time to grow and develop. Keep your eyes on Christ and be patient with yourself.

On this page, write down the most important things you want to remember as you continue your journey from here.

On the following page, create a visual using everything you want to remember as you continue your journey from here.

_____

_____

_____

_____

_____

_____

_____

_____

_____

_____

_____

_____

_____

_____

_____

CONNECT WITH US

OUR MISSION

Our mission is to help girls connect with the River of Life that flows from God and be cultivated into a beautiful pearl.

Through our resources and retreats we mentor girls on how to walk with God, experience freedom, discover their identity, pursue their dreams, and explore creative ways on how their life can make a difference in their community and world in a way that points others to life. We blend the process of spiritual formation and practical life-coaching, guiding girls on their own unique, creative journey of transformation where their faith and life meet.

Visit our website to learn more about us!

- Outreach to children's hospitals
- Events for college age, youth, and children
- River retreats in the mountains of Colorado

Join our online community of girls going through *Cultivating Pearls*!

Website: River and Pearls | RIVERANDPEARLS.ORG

A STORY TO INSPIRE YOU

I WOULD LIKE TO SHARE the story of one of the girls who has gone through the lessons in this book and how her leaves are reaching children in hospitals all over the world and how you may be interested in being part of this beautiful movement.

Morgan is now a freshman in college, but her pearl journey started four years ago, where her story will begin.

Hello, my name is Morgan. When I was a freshman in high school, fifteen years old, I was invited to be part of a group going through the lessons in *Cultivating Pearls*. I wanted to be part of this group so I could learn more about God and how to have a personal relationship with him. The same week I was about to start this group something tragic happened in my family. I lost my little ten-year-old sister from a very brief and tragic battle with leukemia.

Jordyn had a beautiful soul that was unique to her. She was funny, sweet, joyful, and humble. She was so loving and kind to those around her. I loved her caring heart that was expressed frequently throughout her day. Her attitude and actions influenced me to become who I truly am and to be a light for others. There are no words to describe how much I miss her.

The story I am sharing comes from a very deep and personal journey I have been on, and how the lessons in *Cultivating Pearls* came into my life at a time when I needed God the most.

I read a verse that talks about what it is like in heaven and about a beautiful river that flows from God: "Then the angel showed me a river with the water of life, clear as crystal, flowing from the throne of God and of the Lamb" (Revelation 22:1). The verses that followed continued to describe how beautiful heaven is and then ended with an invitation from Jesus to come to this river for healing, for peace, for whatever it is we need.

I closed my eyes and imagined this beautiful place. In my mind's eye, I could see a beautiful blue river flowing from the top of a magnificent mountain range down into a peaceful valley. The warmth of the sun filled this place with comfort. I imagined Jesus by the river.

What at first seemed so very far away began to come closer as I realized that through my faith in Jesus he brings his presence into my heart. It was there I felt him ask me to come on a journey with him.

I started at this peaceful river where we talked about a lot of things and Jesus began to fill my heart with his Spirit. I feel the Holy Spirit is represented by the river that flows down from the top of the mountain. The sound of the trickling water comforted my soul as the Holy Spirit flowed like water into the cracks and crevices of my heart to bring healing and peace. I feel like the Holy Spirit is a good friend, always calling me back, because the river will provide life for my soul.

Jesus then invited me to walk with him, and we started to walk alongside the river and then through the difficult, deeper process of climbing the mountain. The journey of healing was so big, but I took it one step at a time. I feel the mountains represent God, our Father, and they call out to me. He invites me to come and explore and discover new things in my faith. When I do, he gives me a new perspective to help me continue on my journey, even through the unexpected.

When I got to the top of the mountain, the first thing I saw was a glorious sunrise casting light onto the mountain peaks. I feel the sun will always remind me of Jesus, the Son of God. Every morning I look forward to the sun coming out and giving a fresh start to a new day. Whenever I feel sadness start to overtake me, stepping out into the sun fills me with a sense of peace. Though the sadness of losing my sister never goes away, the sun reminds me of the goodness in life and opens my heart to the Lord.

When the comfort of the sun, the call of the mountains, and the healing waters of the river all come together, they remind me of the many experiences that have molded me into who I am as a daughter of God. They also fill my heart with his presence and help me get through difficult days.

As I continued my journey I received a beautiful crown as a symbol that I am a daughter of God. I discovered how to place my roots down deep into his love and explore how the leaves of my tree could bring love to others.

One day as I was having a prayer time, I felt like God whispered in my heart, "Where do you want to go from here?"

"I want to go back down the mountain and help other girls," I said.

I continued to meet with my leader, Christina, for the next three years as part of an internship program with River + Pearls. These years were filled with discovering ways I can shine for other girls and use my creative gifts to help them experience God's love and peace in their own hearts.

I was able to travel to Hawaii and help the leaders of a church use creativity to help girls grow closer to God, lead a summer camp program for young girls in my community, and create a greeting card line that is now sold in retail stores and gift shops as a way to raise funds for my outreach to children.

When I thought about how I could honor Jordyn's life and bring hope to other girls, I thought about all the little girls in the world who are in hospitals, going through difficult experiences. Many people brought coloring books to my little sister when she was in the hospital, but they were often too difficult to do because of how weak she was from her treatments. I had the idea to create a coloring book that would be both inspirational and manageable for the girls.

River + Pearls published the book I created—*My Journey Coloring Book*. Each page has something unique for the children to color that comes from my own personal journey. It is my hope that this book will be their own special book for their own journey and that love will flow from each page.

In a short time, doors started to open at children's hospitals all over the United States. *My Journey Coloring Book* became a tool that hospitals' art therapy departments began using to help children and teens experience healing through art. Coloring each picture is a creative outlet for patients to process emotions, focus on something positive, bring comfort to their hearts, and fill their surroundings with love.

What started as a simple desire to use my gifts to bring hope to others turned into several thousand leaves finding their way into the rooms of children in more hospitals than I could ever have imagined.

I hope that as you open your own heart to the Lord, you will experience his love and guidance. It doesn't mean your journey will be easy, but I believe he will create something more beautiful than you ever thought was possible.

At first, God helped me by coming alongside me to bring healing to my heart. Now I am asking him to flow this healing out of my heart like a beautiful river of life to bring healing to children in hospitals all over the world.

Whoever believes in me, as the Scripture has said, "Out of his heart will flow rivers of living water."

JOHN 7:38, ESV

With love,
Morgan

JOIN THE JOURNEY AND SHINE

for Children in Hospitals in Your Own Community and State

Visit our website to learn more about this opportunity!

River + Pearls | riverandpearls.org

LEADERS GUIDE

CULTIVATING PEARLS was written in a way for each girl to go through on her own, at her own pace, or with a group of friends. The following pages will give you some tips and insight if you are going through the book with a group of friends, or you are leading a group of girls.

BE A PEARL!

> We will not hide these truths from our children; we will tell the next generation about the glorious deeds of the LORD, about his power and his mighty wonders.
>
> PSALM 78:4

Being a pearl is simple. It is coming alongside another girl coming up the road behind you and being a friend. In your own unique way, you will gently and beautifully reflect what God has done in your own life to offer value, hope, and life to the girls. A pearl listens, encourages, shares some of her own story, offers to be a sounding board, and celebrates the lives of the girls God has placed in her life.

Girls and women all over the world are using this book as a tool in journeying alongside other girls. As you work on some of these pages together, it creates an atmosphere of support, understanding, and a natural avenue for the girls to talk about what is going on in their lives.

Thank you for your desire to be a pearl and come alongside the girls in your church, campus, or community! They need you! They are looking for someone like you to shine value into their lives. I have heard it said, *"If you teach a girl a rule, you help her solve a problem. If you teach a girl to walk with God and discover her identity, you help her solve the rest of her life."*

WALKING WITH GOD

Cultivating Pearls helps girls learn how to walk with God in every area of their lives. We present lessons, then ask the girls questions. We then encourage, equip, and empower the girls to go on a journey to discover their answers. The work we do goes deep into the inner workings of their lives. The girls create something meaningful to represent what they have discovered and how the lesson is meaningful to them. This becomes a constant visual reminder, guiding them on their journey of becoming the beautiful pearl God created them to be.

There is a deep rhythm to the way we teach that changes how the girls learn. Once a girl finishes her journey through *Cultivating Pearls*, she takes the tools she learned and applies it to the next season of her journey. One of the main things we hear from girls is how these lessons have changed their life. Not just for now, but for the rest of it. It has given them a new perspective, new tools, and the knowledge of how to apply these tools to their continued spiritual growth.

What Girls Have Said

When we asked several girls to sum up their journey through the book *Cultivating Pearls*, this is what they said:

- Healed
- Changed
- Restored
- New Life
- Inspirational
- Faith

- Transformation
- Forgiven
- Identity
- Anointed
- Growth
- Cultivated

- Unforgettable
- Love
- Shine
- Beautiful

WHO IS THIS BOOK FOR?

This book is for girls of all ages.

Please read the following pages to understand how this book was originally written with college-age girls in mind, but has been a powerful tool for girls of all ages. I will give you tips on the following pages on how to lead the girls you have a heart for, no matter what their ages.

The lessons in this book meet girls where they are. This will make sense to you when you go through a few lessons on your own. Each session shares a Scripture, a lesson, then asks a few questions. The girls then go on a creative journey to answer the question in a way that is unique to them.

College Age

I originally wrote this book with college-age girls in mind for two reasons.

1. I was in college when I first started to learn how to have a relationship with Christ and was ready to go on a journey that requires self-evaluation, processing, and making some hard choices to get where I wanted to be. It was during my college-age years that I was looking for tools to help me grow in my faith and understand how my life could have purpose in God's Kingdom. I did not grow up in a Christian environment, and it wasn't until I was in college that someone shared with me that it was possible to have a relationship with God, and we could get to know him through his Word, the

Bible. If someone had shared with me earlier, I may have been ready. Which is why I think it is important we reach out to girls of all ages.

2. For the past twenty-five years I have been mentoring college-age girls, speaking on college campuses, and at college-age ministry events. The girls are thirsty for a genuine walk with God, and looking for tools that will help them know not only about God, but how to walk with him in a personal way that impacts every part of their life.

All Ages!

Children, elementary, and high school–age girls!

When the college-age girls finished their journeys through *Cultivating Pearls*, they were encouraged at the end of the book to do something to help another girl. Many of them wanted to help girls younger than them, so they started reaching out to high school girls. They wanted the girls to know what they themselves had just learned, because they said it would have helped them so much when they were in high school.

Over the past five years, I have begun to mentor more and more high school girls. They have pleasantly surprised me with how deep they can go when they are ready to make their spiritual growth a priority. The sooner they can make a connection with God, the more tools they will have to navigate their way through the winding roads of peer pressure and identity issues.

When the high school girls ended their journeys through the lessons, they wanted to help the girls younger than them. So we started doing events for middle-school girls, and this past summer we did special day camps for elementary-age girls!

As a leader, you can easily adapt the lessons in this book to the age of the girls you are reaching. You will be amazed at how the younger girls are able to understand things so much better because of the visual elements in the lesson. Keep it simple and ask easy questons that they can understand.

I like to present a lesson, read a verse, ask one question, and let them color the page. Then I like to have the girls talk about what they just colored. This helps them process it and make it personal.

CREATE A SACRED SPACE

Whether you are meeting in a college dorm room, a community center, or a home, I encourage you to take time to create an environment that feels clean, peaceful, inviting, cozy, and safe. Speaking as a leader, I find this can be fun!

When I lead a group of girls in my home, I make sure everything is tidy and warm. I like to have something yummy and healthy baking in the oven, so the house smells good when the girls walk through the front door. I have worship music playing softly in the background. In winter, the fireplace is going. In summer, the back door is open to hear the sound of the water fountain in the garden.

I want the girls to walk in the door and feel like they have been transported to a special sacred space where they can tune out the noise of their lives and spend time with God. When they sit around the living room, their spirits are ready to listen, explore, and grow. Whatever I do, my goal is to make it beautiful for the girls.

Worship Music

Find our playlist for *Cultivating Pearls* on Spotify. We have songs that go with each of the sessions in the book. Search for River + Pearls. I like to have worship music playing softly in the background when the girls arrive and during their creative processing time.

Phones Off and Away

I ask the girls to put their phones in a basket at the front door so they can come into our time together fully present and focused.

Supplies Needed

When I lead a group of girls, I make sure every girl gets a book and a pack of colored pencils. I then put a large bowl on the table filled with colored pencils in every color I can find. I encourage using colored pencils because the color does not bleed through the paper the way markers do.

HOW MANY GIRLS?

This really depends on you and how much space you have for the girls to spread out. This is a personal journey and they like to spread out so no one can look over their shoulder while they are getting their thoughts out. If all the girls in the group are respectful and listen, you can handle more than if you are managing behavior at the same time you are trying to lead.

When I am leading a group of girls in my home, I like to keep it to around twelve girls. When I am leading girls on a college campus setting, at a church, or a retreat setting, I can lead hundreds of girls at a time as long as they have some breathing room to spread out.

What If They Miss a Lesson?

The lessons are carefully structured to build upon each other. If one lesson is missed, it is important for the girls to do it on their own, so they are not behind. Every step of the journey is important, as it all comes together in a beautiful way at the end.

Ask Guiding Questions

I try to never tell the girls what to do. Instead, I guide them to discover what God's Word says by asking them questions that will help them figure it out on their own. This will make it theirs and be life changing for them.

Pay Attention

What the girls create will give you a window into their precious hearts. Pray for wisdom and insight as you gently guide them with truth and love.

Be Patient

The girls are on a journey and it often takes some time for them to discover how to apply the lessons to their lives. Sometimes all you can do is plant a seed and water it through prayer. Sometimes you will see girls' lives transform right before your eyes each week. Every girl comes with a different story and unique background. Love them all. Be patient with every one of them.

WHAT I SHARE WITH THE GIRLS

1. Come as You Are

Wherever you find yourself in your mind or heart or life as you hold this book in your hands, the best place to begin your journey is right where you are. The pages of this book are filled with lessons that will become tools to encourage, empower, and equip you on your journey of learning how to connect with God, grow in your faith, and discover your unique purpose in this world.

2. What You Need

Your Bible, a *Cultivating Pearls* book, a bunch of colored pencils, and a writing pen. In addition to practical items, you will need consistency, an open heart, and desire to grow.

3. Do I Need to Be Creative?

When I use the word *creative*, I am not referring to being an artist. I use the word *creative* to define a unique way of processing your thoughts, ideas, and feelings through words, drawings, and color. I believe we all have a creative outlet but how that flows out of each of us is in a very unique way. So the answer is, you already are creative. This book will inspire you to discover how.

4. Discover

Every lesson is created to flow into the next, bringing the whole journey together in a beautiful way at the end. Everything you do on the way will become your own reflection of discovering how to listen and respond to the truth of God's Word as it transforms your life.

5. Express Yourself

After I share a lesson, I will ask a variety of questions. This is not the kind of book where you just read something and fill in the blank. This is a book of lessons shared and questions asked, and you go on your own personal creative journey to answer them. Some of you may be more inclined to write or journal. I encourage you to also try to sketch something to get a visual to go with your words. Some of you may be more inclined to draw. I encourage you to also add words that describe what you are drawing.

6. Thoughts and Emotions

When we write, we are primarily using our minds to express our thoughts. When we take time to consider what drawing or visual may represent what we are thinking, we tap into our hearts.

7. Transformation in Mind and Heart

When we read a verse of Scripture, it is important to know the truth of what it says so it will transform our minds. When we think about a verse of Scripture and try to come up with a visual way to illustrate the verse and then find ourselves in that picture, it helps the transformation flow into the depths of our hearts as well. My hope is that each of you will not only know about the Kingdom of God, but that the beauty of the Kingdom of God will become the very center of your heart and flow into all the pieces of your life.

8. Revelation 21 and 22

Throughout your journey there will be several times I ask you to reflect on verses in Revelation 21 and 22.

EXAMPLE OF TIME LINE

WHEN I AM LEADING A GROUP OF GIRLS that come each week, I like to do it from 6:30 p.m. to 9:00 p.m. That gives them time to grab dinner before heading over. I call my style of leading "structurally rhythmic." I make it feel like it easily flows from one thing to the next, but in my mind I have a certain time line for everything, so I make sure to accomplish my goals for the girls by the end of our time. It flows something like this:

6:30–6:45
Connection Time

I put upbeat worship music on. I welcome the girls as they come in and let them talk with each other and have fun chatting. I have Trader Joe's Kettle Corn Popcorn out in a large bowl on the counter. I have picked up some cute little tin buckets at Hobby Lobby and I have written each girl's name on a trendy label and put it on the container, so she would have her own popcorn stash by her side throughout the night.

While they visit around the island in my kitchen, I make smoothies for them and have some cookies baking in the oven. This creates a fun and homey way to start and gives the girls time to get their mind ready for our session.

6:45–7:15
Lesson Time

All music off. The girls gather in the living room with me while I share the lesson and have a few minutes for them to ask any questions they may have.

7:15–8:15
Creative Time

I put quiet, peaceful worship music on, and the girls spread out and have quiet time to process how they feel, and what they are thinking about the message

I shared. I leave them with a few questions to ponder. They think about how they would like to create something that helps them document and express what they are feeling and thinking. The book guides them through this process. The girls then spread out at tables or sit on the floor and they work on the pages in their book that go with the message I shared. During this time, I pay close attention to what each girl is doing so I can offer guidance.

8:15–8:45

Share Time, Question and Answer, Closing Prayer

This is a very personal journey, so I only encourage the girls who feel comfortable to share. This is a good time to let the girls ask questions and share some of your own story in your answers. End with a prayer over the girls.

8:45–9:00

Clean Up

Thank you for your willingness to take time out of your busy life to help our next generation of girls learn how to walk with God! May your life be blessed as you join God in bringing love and life to the girls in your community!

With love, Christina

BUT THEN I RECALL

ALL YOU HAVE DONE, O LORD;

I REMEMBER YOUR

wonderful deeds

OF LONG AGO.

Psalm 77:11

The Bible tells us many stories where a symbol was used to help the people of God remember what God had done on their behalf.

I pray that as you are finishing your journey through *Cultivating Pearls,* you will connect with us and continue to grow as a beautiful pearl! As you decide to follow Jesus, I pray that you will always see his light and know which way to go. "I will instruct you and teach you in the way you should go; I will counsel you with my eye upon you" (Psalm 32:8, ESV).

He will always guide you and shine his light through you. As you have received your crown, I pray you will allow the Holy Spirit to "set you apart" and live a holy life within the boundaries of God's Kingdom. He is calling his girls to take their place. You are not alone. I hope you will join our hands as we form a circle around the world to help other girls find their way to the River of Life as you have. May God bless you as you look to him for all your needs.

With love,

Rachel, a college student leader

OUR PEARL NECKLACE
CONNECTS US!

GIRLS ALL OVER THE WORLD are wearing our necklace featuring a solitary pearl on a genuine Greek leather cord.

I originally received this necklace as a gift from a girl in Texas who had been touched by a pearl lesson I taught several years ago. I love the necklace so much I wear it every day! Every morning I take my pearl necklace from the special place where I keep it, put it around my neck while looking in the mirror and say, "My name is Christina. I belong to God."

So many girls I met were drawn to the necklace that I began to buy them as gifts. I encouraged the girls to wear the necklace as a reminder of all the lessons I had taught them about being a pearl and what it represented to them on their journey with God.

I noticed that everyone I gave the necklace to never took it off. The necklace became something that reminded them of who they are in God's eyes, just as it did for me.

We now carry the necklaces in our online store so everyone can wear one! This is also a really special way of blessing another girl and telling her she is a pearl of much value. She will never take it off and never forget you for calling out her value and worth.

River + Pearls | riverandpearls.org

ABOUT THE AUTHOR

CHRISTINA DiMARI is the author of four books that encourage, equip, and empower girls to develop a personal relationship with God, live whole lives, pursue their dreams, and use their gifts to shine for others. She is an ordained chaplain, earning her bachelor's in biblical theology from Simpson University, and is certified in art therapy. Christina currently leads a nonprofit organization she founded called River + Pearls, hosts retreats by a beautiful blue river in the mountains of Colorado, and teaches spiritual formation and leadership training to high school and college-age students and staff. Her work and outreach have been featured in numerous magazines, including *Today's Christian Woman*, *Life Beautiful*, *In Touch*, *Radiant*, *Australia Girls*, and *Women's SurfStyle* magazine. Christina and her husband have two adventurous sons and enjoy family time and their passion for fly-fishing.